ROLOFF BENY

The Romance of Architecture

With an Introduction by

JOHN JULIUS NORWICH

AND AN ANTHOLOGY
DRAWN FROM ARCHITECTURAL
WRITERS AND TRAVELLERS
FROM VITRUVIUS
TO SACHEVERELL SITWELL

HARRY N. ABRAMS, INC.,
PUBLISHERS, NEW YORK

Endpapers: Detail of the doorway of S. Michele, Pavia, Italy
Half title: Round window from the Romanesque abbey of Pomposa, Italy
Pages 2–3. Portal ceiling of the Friday Mosque, Yazd, Iran
Frontispiece. Pierced marble screen in the Red Fort, Delhi, India

Thanks are due to Signora Antonella Carini of the Studio Beny in Rome for her invaluable help in the selection of the pictures and provision of information for the captions and notes.

Library of Congress Catalog Card Number: 85–71001
ISBN 0–8109–1589–8

© 1985 THAMES AND HUDSON LTD, LONDON

PHOTOGRAPHS © THE ESTATE OF ROLOFF BENY, 1985

Published in 1985 by Harry N. Abrams, Incorporated, New York

Printed and bound in Japan

CONTENTS

The Romance of Architecture

INTRODUCTION

WHEN ROLOFF BENY died at his home on the banks of the Tiber on 16 March 1984, at the age of only sixty, the world lost one of the most imaginative and dramatic of its architectural photographers. Not that his work was exclusively concerned with architecture; Roloff could discern – and capture – the poetry of a floating leaf, a laughing child or an old armchair just as surely as that of a moss-covered temple or a fallen entablature. But buildings, as he once told me, were his special love; and he gave expression to that love, in one glorious volume after another, throughout his life.

Fortunately, both for us and for him, he left in his studio immense quantities of photographs, many of which had never seen the light of day; his friends and publishers have thus been able to continue work on the various projects in which he was engaged at the time of his death. Of these projects, the most ambitious was the one he called his *Visual Journals*, which he conceived as a photographic trilogy: the opening volume he intended to be, very properly, a distillation of his thoughts on architecture, the second was to be concerned with the beauties of nature, while the last he planned to devote to his fellow men. Together the three were to constitute what would be, in effect, his testament – a final summation, and celebration, of the world as he saw it. The first part of that trilogy you now hold in your hands.

9

*Detail of reliefs by Lorenzo Maitani on
the west front of Orvieto Cathedral,
Italy*

It is an unusual task, and a difficult one, to produce another man's testament, even when he has given clear and cogent ideas of the form that it should take; and it may well be that Roloff, had he lived, would have arranged his material somewhat otherwise. I should have been astonished, however, if he had decided on any radical difference of approach. For he was not only a highly intelligent man; he was also remarkably articulate, and certainly not one to leave his friends in any doubt of his thoughts and opinions – least of all on subjects about which he felt so passionately. Those who have put together this book in his memory knew him well and worked with him often; they have been acutely aware of their responsibility and have discharged it faithfully and conscientiously. Roloff, I believe, would have genuinely admired what they have done. He would also have been deeply grateful.

Here, then, is a collection of magnificent architectural photographs by a master of the *genre*, grouped not (as collections of this kind usually are) by place, period or style, but according to specific elements of construction. Some of these elements – walls, doors, windows – are necessities, common to virtually all buildings, whatever and wherever they may be; others – columns, towers, domes – being at least partly decorative, are somewhat less universal. All, however, are basic architectural components, susceptible of infinite variation but to be found, in one form or another, across the entire globe.

Now more often than not, when we look at a building, we accept these components – unless they are in some way unusual or impinge particularly on our notice – only as parts of the whole structure; we are unable, as it were, to see the trees for the wood. One of the objects of this book is to focus our attention instead on these individual elements, to oblige us to think for a moment what each one is, what purpose it serves, what qualities it requires and of what stylistic variations it is capable. Only then, Roloff believed, shall we fully understand the contribution that it makes to the *ensemble*.

Exercises of this kind are more essential to the appreciation of architecture than to that of any other art form, and for one very simple reason: there is too much of it. We see it everywhere, all around us, all the time. And because by far the greater part of it happens to be bad architecture we develop, in sheer self-defence, a measure of blindness to it that enables us to get through our lives with a minimal degree of visual suffering. This, quite obviously, is as it should be; but it is equally important that we should be able to resharpen our sensibilities whenever we need to do so, and that is where the exercises come in. Faced with an interesting building that I have never seen – or at least thought about – before, I personally have a whole series of questions which I make a point of asking myself. What material is it made of? Is that material right for it? Does the building adequately serve the purpose for which it was designed? How good is the workmanship? What about the windows? Are they the right size and shape, and are they properly spaced? Is the whole structure properly proportioned, or does it look squat or spindly? And so the self-interrogation goes on, invariably ending with the most important question of all: do I like it?

There are plenty of other exercises, too, if one has the time; a particularly enjoyable one, for me, is to try and discover at least three interesting or amusing details which I should certainly have missed had I not been on the lookout for them. But all this, of course, is more of a game than anything else – and a game which everyone can play in his own way. The secret of success in it was best summed up by John Ruskin. 'Don't look at buildings,' he wrote, '*watch* them.'

This advice apart, there are I believe only two unalterable rules which must be observed if humanly possible; first, never content yourself with looking simply at the show front of a building. Walk all the way round it; only then will you have a hope of finding its true character. Second – and more important still – avoid all temptation to take a photograph for at least five minutes. How sadly familiar to us all is the tourist who snaps away for all he is worth at a masterpiece that he may have travelled half the world to see, but who apparently prefers to look at a minuscule reflection of it in a tiny viewfinder than to raise his eyes to the real thing – and how often, one wonders, does he even look at the photograph afterwards?

Great architecture is not to be conceived of in terms of apertures or shutter speeds – and Roloff knew it. He would stand and stare, motionless, sometimes for ten minutes or more; then he would begin to prowl, first exploring the building itself until he felt he understood it, and only then starting to think about how he was going to capture its essence on film. It was a time-consuming technique and often an extremely exhausting one, not only for Roloff but also for those who accompanied him on his journeys; the results, however, speak for themselves.

Which being so, it follows that the photographs in this book have no real need for an accompanying essay. Instead, the publishers have had the idea of complementing them with an anthology – a collection of thoughts, aphorisms and even occasional verses on the subject of architecture, together with accounts of some of the buildings illustrated, by explorers and early writers. These too will give us cause to reflect; and it is as well that they should, for this most indispensable of the arts tends all too easily to be taken for granted – and for the very reason of its indispensability, for, unlike painting, sculpture or music, architecture is quite literally essential to life. Without it, we should die of exposure. This indisputable fact should, one might have thought, induce us to value it more, rather than less; but human nature, alas, is not like that. The practical, utilitarian side of architecture has always militated against it, preventing it from receiving that last ounce of respect that is its due.

And so, if we are to get something more than simple enjoyment out of these astonishing photographs, we must not just look at them; we must also think about what it is that we are looking at, reflecting for a moment on the nature of doors or windows, arches or staircases, the reasons for their existence, the various forms they can take, the extent to which their decoration is dictated by their function, and any other similar questions that may occur to us. In doing so we shall learn much; and we shall also gain a new insight into what made Roloff Beny the great photographer he was.

JOHN JULIUS NORWICH

Early Christian relief (c. 7th century) used as an altar tomb at Sta Maria del Priorato, Rome

+ ET SANGVINEM SCI SEBA + ET RELIQVIE SCIQ VADRAG
STIANI MAR ET RELIQVIE SCIA BVNDINIAR
+ HI C R E CONDITVM EST CAPVT G SAVIN
SPOLITINI E P ET MAR G T COSTA SCESAR

I WALLS
THE SURFACE AND THE DOOR

THE WALL is both a barrier and a protection. From the outside its character is one of exclusion, and at its simplest – in town-walls, the walls of castles or of prisons – this is its dominant purpose. But in most buildings, this impression is softened by articulation – by the lines of buttresses or string-courses, by the placing of openings and by decorative features that break up and impose pattern upon the surface. From the inside, a wall expresses security and defence. But again, this sense of enclosure is usually softened by the use of line and colour – by hangings, furnishings and the paraphernalia of every-day life that may hide the wall altogether.

Architects themselves do not dwell much on the qualities of walls as such. The rich variety and attractive textures of wood, stone, brick and plaster are things that we associate more with vernacular buildings than with sophisticated design, though occasionally the two have come together. Ruskin makes the point that the wall is to the architect what the canvas is to the painter, and the architects bear this out. Concentrating on their creative effort, they take the medium for granted.

Detail of the Palazzo dei Diamanti, Ferrara, Italy

Cumae, the Sybil's cave

A spacious cave, within its farmost part,
Was hewed and fashioned by laborious art,
Through the hill's hollow sides; before the place,
A hundred doors a hundred entries grace;
As many voices issue, and the sound
Of Sybil's words as many times rebound.

Virgil, 'Aenead' (Dryden's translation)

1   Part of the subterranean labyrinth that formed
     the dwelling of the legendary sybil of Cumae,
     Italy.
2   Ruins of the Greek fortifications of Euryelus,
     near Syracuse in Sicily.
3   The Lion Gate, Mycenae, Greece.
4   The *tholos*, Epidauros, Greece.
5   The Temple of Khnum, Elephantine Island,
     Aswan, Egypt.
6   Curtain separating the sanctuary from the
     hypostyle hall of the great temple of Amun,
     Karnak, Egypt.
7   'Cube of Zoroaster', Naqsh-e Rustam, Iran.

2

3

4

The 'Cube of Zoroaster' revalued

This is real architecture; or perhaps one should say, since its function has no relation to its form, that it represents a real architectural tradition of which we are otherwise ignorant. It is a copy of a house. Where was that house? In Persia? It gives no hint of that expensive, cross-bred sophistication about to blossom at Persepolis. If it stood in a Mediterranean country, it would be hailed as the original source of domestic architecture in quattrocento Italy and Georgian England. Unlike the Greek temple, which developed out of a wooden form concerned with the stress of weights, this tombhouse derives from a form of brick or mud conveying an idea of content; its beauty is in the spacing of ornament on a flat wall. It is surprising to find this principle, on which all good domestic building since the Renascence has depended, fully stated in Persia about the middle of the sixth century BC. It is equally surprising to remember how little attention, from this point of view, visitors to Naksh-i-Rustam have so far given it.

Robert Byron, 'The Road to Oxiana', 1937

The Lion Gate before Schliemann

Crossing a barren valley, I saw the ruins of Mycenae on the side of a facing hill. I particularly admired one of the gates of the city fashioned out of gigantic blocks of stone that are set on the rock of the mountain itself and seem to form part of it. Two colossal lions carved on each side of the gate are its only ornament; these are represented in relief and stand on their hind legs looking outwards, like the lions which support the coats of arms of our knights of old. The heads of the lions are missing. Not even in Egypt have I seen such imposing architecture, and the desert which surrounds it adds still further to its grandeur.

François René de Chateaubriand, 'Itinéraire de Paris à Jérusalem', 1811

8, 9 Temple of Bacchus, Baalbek, Lebanon.

The basic element

Now it does not seem to me sufficiently recollected that a wall surface is to an architect what a white canvas is to a painter with only this difference, that the wall has already a sublimity in its height, substance and other character, on which it is more dangerous to break than to touch with shade the canvas surface. And, for my part, I think a smooth, broad, freshly laid surface of gesso a fairer thing than most pictures I see painted on it; much more a noble surface of stone than most architectural features which it is caused to assume.

John Ruskin, 'The Seven Lamps of Architecture', 1849

The 'dead' wall

A wall has no business to be dead. It ought to have members in its make, and purposes in its existence, like an organized creature, and to answer its ends in a living and energetic way; and it is only when we do not choose to put any strength or organization into it, that it offends us by its deadness. Every wall ought to be a 'sweet and lovely wall'.

John Ruskin, 'The Stones of Venice', 1851

Walls in perspective

It ought to be observed, that walls should diminish in proportion as they rise; therefore those which appear above ground must be half as thick as the walls in the foundation; those of the second storey half a brick thinner than the walls of the first; and in this manner to the top of the building; but with discretion, that the upper part be not too thin.

Andrea Palladio, 'Quattro Libri dell' Architettura', 1570

An architect's creed

Above all, we should show the naked wall in all its sleek beauty.

Hendrik Berlage, 'Gedenken über Stil in der Baukunst', 1905

26

Greek and Roman walls

Our Roman workmen, in their hurry to finish, devote themselves only to the facings of the walls, setting them upright but filling in the space between them with broken stones and mortar thrown in anyhow. This makes three different sections in the same structure: two consisting of facing and one of filling between them. The Greeks, however, do not build so; but laying their stones level and building every other stone lengthwise into the thickness, they do not fill the space between, but construct the thickness of their walls in one solid and unbroken mass from the facings to the interior. Further, at intervals they lay single stones which run through the entire thickness of the wall. These stones, which show at each end, add very greatly to the solidity of the walls.

Vitruvius, 'De Architectura', 1st century AD

The wall organized

One can look at the exterior of a building simply as a composition of solids and voids, to be judged purely in terms of abstract patterns, irrespective of the needs or requirements of the interior. Some architectural rules are prescribed by the laws of physics. Others depend on a sense of what is fitting and the right relation of one part to another. Such proportions will be approved by every eye no matter how little practised in such matters.

Quatremère de Quincy, 'Dictionaire historique d'Architecture', 1832

Indoor scenery

Wall-surfaces make our indoor scenery and are often required to do no more. They also provide the only vertical plane we have constantly before our eyes, and may be used for the display of things that otherwise must be stored and perhaps forgotten or mislaid. Again, they can give prominence to writing whether edifying, like mottoes, or cautionary, like 'Shut the Door' or 'Mene, mene, tekel upharsin.' They can hold up bookshelves, they can provide a field for paintings, they can be dissimulated with mirrors.

H. S. Goodhart-Rendel, 'Vitruvian Nights', 1932

The spell of Angkor

Since the discovery of Angkor, many volumes and many articles have appeared, most of them conceived in poetic excitement and achieving romantic inexactitude. Almost everyone who has seen these prestigious prodigies becomes temporarily an intoxicated poet. The Chinese ambassador with his golden city and the great burnished lotus flower that blazed like a beacon on the highest tower of Bayon; the French naturalist who rhapsodized over the startling vision five centuries later; Pierre Loti, who described it with a felicitous beauty even greater than his normal lushness; nearly all the twentieth-century travellers, who fall suddenly into enchantment, intoxicated by the delirious maze that piles its complications to the sky, by the stone city and its palaces and temples foundered in the engulfing forest. Pierre Loti saw a picture of it as a child; great strange towers entwined with exotic branches, and knew that he would one day see them. When he did so, in middle age, the colossal temple seemed, in the hot glare of noon, like a mirage. It took a little time before he was caught in its spell, wandering enchanted and bemused through the maze of courts, terraces, corridors, twisting stairways, between walls carved with long processions of dancing Apsaras, lovely in their smiling grace, and battling chariots and elephants, and always the musing god, cross-legged and calm. To enter the great temple by causeway and lilied moat was to be caught into some delirious dream; by night a dream of darkness, wandering through endless galleries, climbing spiralling stairs grown with grass and slippery with centuries of feet, past great towered and arcaded terraces, tree-grown, one terrace above another till from the summit he looked down on the roof of forest that waved over Angkor Thom.

Rose Macaulay, 'Pleasure of Ruins', 1953

16

17

23

24

25

26

An English architect at S. Zeno, Verona

A longish walk through squalid suburbs leads us to the open space in front of the noble basilica of S. Zenone; it is a desolate waste-looking space, and the poor, old, uneared-for church looks now as though its day was well-nigh past; as if neglect and apathy were all that men could give now where once they were wont to lavish so much of their treasure and love and art. . . . There is a grand west doorway, full of noble and elaborate sculpture, having round the arch representations of the signs of the various months of the year, with detached shafts standing out on monsters and supporting a low canopy. The doors themselves are of bronze, very elaborate and of great interest, owing to their excessively early date and good character.

G. E. Street, 'Brick and Marble in the Middle Ages', 1855

At S. Michele, Pavia

From the cathedral we found our way to S. Michele, a very celebrated church, but more interesting to an antiquary in search of curiosities than to an architect in search of the beautiful. The west end is very curious, and has a succession of sculptures, introduced in the most eccentric manner, and with but little method in their arrangement. There are three western doorways, and all of them are elaborately ornamented with carvings.

G. E. Street, 'Brick and Marble in the Middle Ages', 1855

29 Doorway in Kairouan, Tunisia.

WALLS
THE FACADE AND ITS OPENINGS

THE FOCAL POINTS OF A WALL are the openings in it. In all architecture, it is the windows and doors which have been singled out for emphasis. Their relative sizes, their degree of ornamentation and their disposition give expression to a façade in much the same way as eyes and mouth give expression to a face. Buildings can smile, can frown or can sulk. A doorway can welcome the visitor or reject him. The door itself, which is always meant to be seen shut, is invariably a rejection; the act of opening it, an invitation. Windows are like two-way mirrors, through which the inhabitants of the house can observe without being observed. Often this is made explicit by curtains or screens, separating two spaces and conferring privilege upon one of them.

Windows and doors assume particular importance in Gothic architecture, the period during which they attained their richest forms and their most expressive meaning. For the architects of the Age of Reason, practical consideration came uppermost, until by our own time the window is merely a tiresomely unpredictable means of ventilation.

Window in the Tempio Malatestiano, Rimini, Italy, with relief sculpture by Agostino di Duccio. Mid 15th century

A masterpiece of Renaissance Spain

Continuing past the enormous and theatrical Seminario Conciliar, with its splendid interior courts or cloisters, we come to the Casa de las Conchas, of pure fantasy yet one of the most 'Spanish' things in Spain. Its exterior, as the name portends, is studded with carved scallop shells, a form of decoration that is, after all, no more unreasonable than the rustication of the Palazzo Strozzi in Florence, one of the admitted masterworks of the Italian Renaissance. If the Casa de las Conchas was really completed in 1483 and not, as some authorities would have it, in 1514, it antedated its Florentine equivalent. Moreover, its wrought iron lanterns and lovely triple window grille might be held to surpass in beauty the more famous *fanali* or corner lanterns of the Palazzo Strozzi, which are among the most celebrated instances of Italian ironwork of the time. The window grilles have been conceived especially for the shadows that they throw, which are like so many intricate cages hanging on the golden stone.

Sacheverell Sitwell, 'Spain', 1950

30   Interior of the so-called Temple of Diana at Nîmes, France.
31   Tomb of Xerxes, Naqsh-e Rustam, Iran.
32   Palermo Cathedral, Sicily.
33   Palazzo dei Diamanti, Ferrara, Italy.
34   Casa de las Conchas, SAlamanca, Spain.
35   Gaur, India.
36   The side wall of Orvieto Cathedral, Italy.

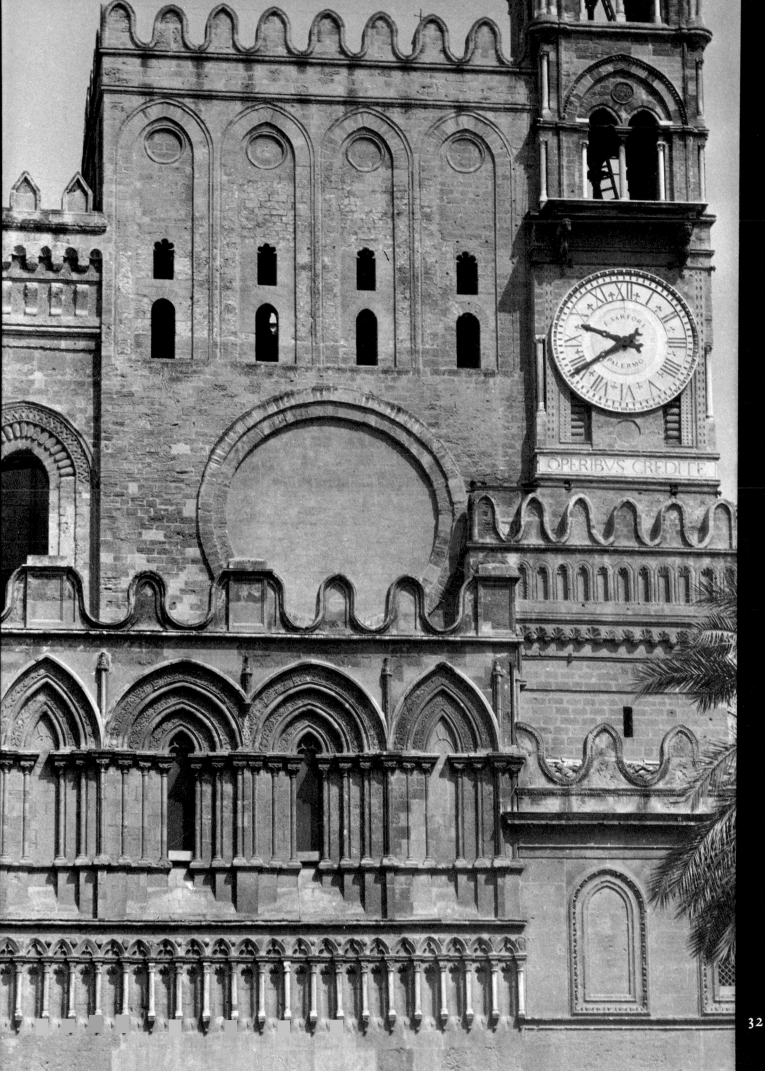

34

Gaur in romantic ruin

Many abandoned cities, such as Gaur and Pandúa in Bengal, Mandu and Chandravati in Central India, and probably hundreds more, have gone down into the jungle, some to be recovered in our present age of tenderness to ancient ruins, others to be lost for ever. Gaur, one of the most magnificent in India (which is to say in the world), was, both before and after its Mohammedan conquest in 1198, the capital of Bengal, a celebrated city of beautiful buildings and high learning, splendidly walled, ten miles long, with great stone embankments. Its huge brick citadel, set with four corner towers and gate, now encloses desolation. The Golden Mosque, with arcaded corridor and brick domes, has been long since wrecked by trees growing up between its bricks, tearing it to pieces; other smaller but delightful mosques are also partly shattered; their courts grown with trees. The tall minaret, from which the muezzin was called, stands erect, shrub-grown, broken-domed; the immense walls of the palace look, in the nineteenth-century pictures, like vertical forests, a-sprout with trees; they would make easy climbing. The Dakhill Gate, in the same pictures, also supports a grove of trees on its square lintel. Broken marbles and fragments lie everywhere.

Rose Macaulay, 'Pleasure of Ruins', 1953

Intimations of the Gothic Revival

But how shall I describe Netley to you? I can only do so by telling you that it is the spot in the world for which Mr Chute and I wish. The ruins are vast, and retain fragments of beautiful fretted roofs pendent in the air, with all variety of Gothic patterns of windows wrapped round and round with ivy – many trees are sprouted up against the walls, and only want to be increased with cypresses! A hill rises above the Abbey, encircled with wood: the fort, in which we would build a tower for habitation, remains with two small platforms. This little castle is buried from the Abbey in a wood, in the very centre, on the edge of the hill: on each side breaks in the view of the Southampton sea, deep blue, glistening with silver and vessels.

Horace Walpole, Letter to Richard Bentley, September 1755

37   Netley Abbey, Hampshire.

Against niches

What in effect is a niche? What use is it? In truth I know none. I cannot believe that good sense can be pleased with looking on a statue in a window cut as a hollow tower. My antipathy to niches is invincible, and till they have shown me the principle and necessity of it, I shall lay violent hands on all those who shall present them.

Abbé Laugier, 'Essai sur l'Architeture', 1753

Into the infinite

When windows were in practice indispensible, they were for the sake of artistic expression concealed by galleries as in the Eastern basilica. The window as architecture, on the other hand, is peculiar to the Faustian soul and the most significant symbol of its depth-experience. In it can be felt the will to emerge from the interior into the boundless.

Oswald Spengler, 'The Decline of the West', 1918

North and South

You probably have a distinct idea – those of you at least who are interested in architecture – of the shape of the windows in Westminster Abbey, in the Cathedral of Chartres, or in the Duomo of Milan. Can any of you, I should like to know, make a guess at the shape of the windows in the Sistine Chapel, the Stanze of the Vatican, the Scuola di San Rocco or the lower church of Assisi? The soul or anima of the first three buildings is in their windows; but of the last four in their walls.

John Ruskin, 'Val d'Arno', 1886

The shapes of windows

Window apertures, as compared with door apertures, have almost infinite licence of form and size; they may be of any shape, from the slit or cross to the circle; of any size from the loophole of the castle to the pillars of light of the cathedral apse.

John Ruskin, 'The Stones of Venice', 1851

Façade of a house at Bressanone, Italy

The Piazza of Vigevano

Ludovico [il Moro] is trying very hard to beautify Vigevano and to make it into a city; in the vicinity of the castle he has torn down a rather wide street of houses to make way for a beautiful, wide and very long square with arcades, columns and arches surrounded by shops. When it is completed it will be a beautiful and magnificent thing.

Ferrarese ambassador, August 1494

38 South transept of Melrose Abbey, Scotland.

39 A 19th-century house in Valencia, Spain.

40 Detail of the tomb of Sheikh Safi at Ardabil, Iran.

41 Façade of the church of S. Croce in Gerusalemme, Rome.

42 Painted decoration in the Renaissance Piazza Ducale of Vigevano, north Italy.

43 Façade of Siena Cathedral, Italy.

44 Central pediment of the façade of S. Michele, Lucca, Italy.

45 A girl looks from the latticed window of an old house in North India.

46 The back view of the façade of S. Michele, Lucca, Italy, a false front corresponding to nothing inside the church.

47 Façade of the Breganze House, Piombino d'Ese, Italy.

48 Central part of the façade of S. Pablo, Valladolid, Spain.

49 Interior of the Friday Mosque, Isfahan, Iran.

50 Detail of the pulpit, Great Mosque of Kairouan, Tunisia.

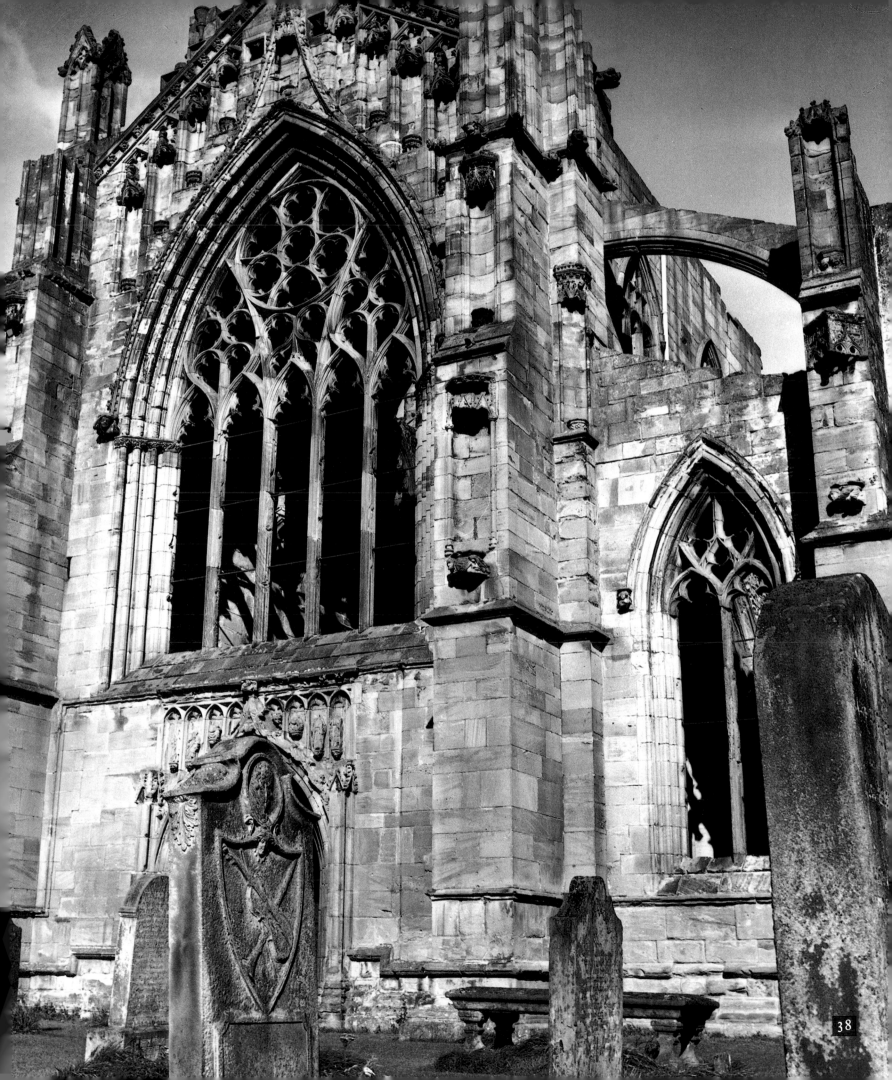

39

40

41

42

44

45

46

47

Human scale

Naturally, the shape and size of human beings remain the basic factors in deciding the form and proportions of openings. If certain Chinese designs present us with doors whose openings consist of a perfect circle, we regard these only as one of these exceptions which far from disproving the rule, prove only that in architecture there is nothing founded upon the principle of common sense which may not somewhere be contradicted by facts at variance with usage and reason.

Quatremère de Quincy 'Dictionnaire historique d'Architecture', 1832

Ill-formed doors

The ancients sometimes made their doors, and even their windows, narrower at the top than at the bottom. This oddity has been very little practiced by the modern artists. Scamozzi disapproves of it; so do several other writers, and it is a matter of surprise that a person of such refined taste as the Earl of Burlington should have introduced a couple of these ill-formed doors in the *cortile* of his house in Picadilly. It must, however, be allowed that they, like some other uncouth things, have one valuable property – that they shut themselves; which in a country where neither man nor woman takes thought or trouble about shutting doors after them, deserves its praise, and was perhaps, the original cause of their introduction among the ancients.

Sir William Chambers, 'Treatise on Civil Architecture', 1759

51   Part of the west front of the church of La
     Merced in Antigua, Guatemala.

*Side elevation of Ferrara Cathedral,
Italy. 13th century*

70

Perfection at Isfahan

The two dome-chambers of the Friday Mosque . . . were built about the same time, at the end of the eleventh century. In the larger, which is the main sanctuary of the mosque, twelve massive piers engage in a Promethean struggle with the weight of the dome. Contrast this with the smaller chamber, which is really a tomb-tower incorporated in the mosque. The inside is roughly thirty feet square and sixty high; its volume is perhaps one third of the other's. But while the larger lacked the experience necessary to its scale, the smaller embodies that precious moment between too little experience and too much, when the elements of construction have been refined of superfluous bulk, yet still withstand the allurements of superfluous grace; so that each element, like the muscles of a trained athlete, performs its function with winged precision, not concealing its effort, as over-refinement will do, but adjusting it to the highest degree of intellectual meaning. This is the perfection of architecture, attained not so much by the form of the elements – for this is a matter of convention – but by their chivalry of balance and proportion. And this small interior comes nearer to that perfection than I would have thought possible outside classical Europe.

Robert Byron, 'The Road to Oxiana', 1937

58

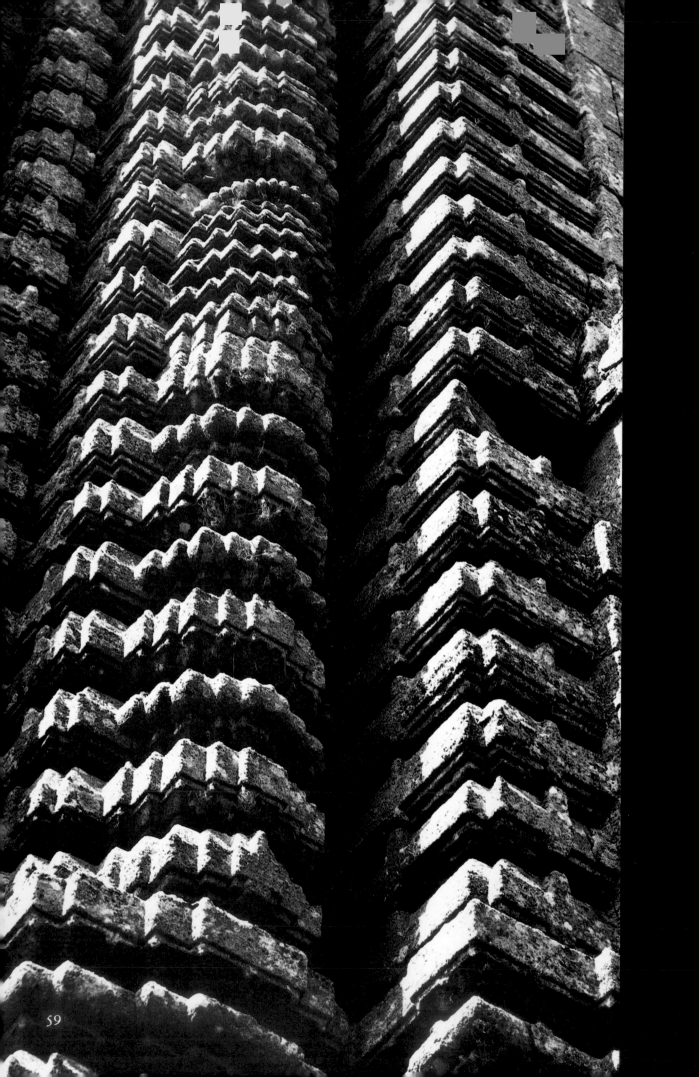

61

62

The placing of windows

No room ought to be without a window, by which the enclosed air may be let out and renewed, because else it will corrupt and grow unwholesome ... The windows will be best contrived for admitting the sun if they are made large, and yet may avoid being troubled by the winds at the same time if we place them high, so that the cold air may not blow directly upon the people within. Lastly, from whatever side we take in the light, we ought to make such an opening for it as may always give us free sight of the sky, and the top of the opening ought never to be too low, because we are to see the light with our eyes and not with our heels.

Leon Battista Alberti, 'De re aedificatoria', 1485

Where do draughts come from?

Our neighbours across the street live in a Texas Cape Cod, one of those houses with a crew haircut – no overhangs. They are not very sociable except on rainy days when they almost smother to death, and then I guess they take the lesser of two evils and come to see us so they can get cool, because we can keep most of our windows open because of the overhangs. In the case of one of those overhangs, when it rains we do have to close those windows. Being a typical architect I got curious so I bought a smoke candle and lit it to try to trace the airflow pattern around this particular overhang. I held it up; swish! boy, she went right in. I moved it six inches; wow, she turned around and went the other way; so right now I don't know whether I am getting air in any of the windows.

W. W. Caudill, Research Architect with the Texas Engineering Experiment Station, College Station, Texas, 1960s

62 A window in the Alhambra, Granada, Spain.

II COLUMNS AND COLONNADES

ANY POST CAN SUPPORT WEIGHT. A column is a consciously shaped expression of that support. All styles of architecture have found ways of achieving this expression, but it was the Greeks who succeeded most triumphantly. For the very beginning, the three main classical orders – Doric, Ionic and Corinthian – were seen as semi-human in their proportions and degrees of strength. The slight swelling in the centre of the column (entasis) gave the impression that the stone was actually compressed under the weight it bore.

In defining the different characters of the three orders, Renaissance writers took their cue from Vitruvius, but indulged in even more fanciful imagery. One of the most popular allegorical texts, the *Hypnerotomachia Poliphili* takes architectural symbolism to extremes, in language that is virtually impossible to turn into clear sense. Such poetic licence stands in striking contrast to the apologists of the Enlightenment, for whom the orders embodied rational order.

Colonnade in the Roman city of Jerash, Libya

The Temple of Apollo at Bassae

It is impossible to give an idea of the romantic beauty of the situation of the temple. It stands on a high ridge looking over lofty barren mountains and an extensive country below them. The ground is rocky, thinly patched with vegetation, and spotted with splendid ilexes. The view gives one Ithome, the stronghold and last defence of the Messenians against Sparta, to the south-west; Arcadia, with its many hills, to the east; and to the south the range of Taygetus with still beyond them the sea.

C. R. Cockerell, Travel Diary, August 1811

The origins of Doric and Ionic

The first temple, dedicated to Apollo, was built after the manner of those they had seen in Achaia, which they called Doric, because temples of the same sort had been erected in the cities of the Dorians. But some time after that – building a temple to Diana, different from these and of a more delicate structure; being formed upon the proportions of the female body, as Doric had been upon those of a robust man; and adorning the capitals of their columns with volutes, to represent the curls of a woman's hair, and the shafts with flutings, to express the folds of her garment – they gave to this second manner of building the name of Ionic, because it was invented and first used by the Ionians.

Vitruvius, 'De Architectura', 1st century AD

The lascivious Corinthian

The Corinthian is a column lasciviously decked, like a wanton courtesan. Its proportions are elegant in the extreme; every part of the order is divided into a great variety of members and abundantly enriched with a variety of ornaments, and therein much participating, as all inventions do, of the place where they were first born; Corinth having been without controversy one of the wantonest towns in the world.

Sir Henry Wotton, 'The Elements of Architecture', 1624

The column's destiny

Follow out the destiny of the column, from the Egyptian tomb-temple in which columns are ranked to mark the path for the traveller, through the Doric peripteros in which they are held together by the body of the building and the early Arabian basilica where they support the interior, to the façades of the Renaissance in which they provide the upward-striving element.

Oswald Spengler, 'The Decline of the West', 1918

69   Court of the Lions, Alhambra, Granada, Spain.

Architectural allegory

The two straight pillars of seven diameters upon either of the aforementioned stilipodes and square altars did stretch upward of a pumish or tawny colour, the outside shining clear and smoothly polished, chamfered and channelled with four and twenty rebatements or channels in every column betwixt the nextruls or cordels. Of these the third part was round, and the reason of their cutting in such sort (that is, two parts chamfered and the third round) as I thought was this: the frame or temple was dedicated to both sexes, that is, to a god and a goddess, or to the mother and the son, or to the husband and the wife, or the father and the daughter and such like. And therefore the expert and cunning workmen in the elder time for the feminine sex, did use more channelling and chamfering and double variety than for the masculine, because of their slippery and unconstant nature. The cause of so much rebating was to show that this was the temple of a goddess, for chamfering doth set forth the plaits of feminine apparel, upon the which they placed a chapter [capital] with prependant folding, like unto plaited and curled hair, and feminine dressing and sometimes instead of a chapter a woman's head with crisped hair.

Francesco Colonna, 'Hypnerotomachia Poliphili', 1499

The characters of Doric and Ionic

Grave and simple in its design and general proportions, the Doric order presents a similar gravity and simplicity in its smallest details; effect is obtained by the contours, the outlines, the play of light and shade upon large surfaces, and by the form of the mouldings. The Ionic order, on the other hand, elegant in its general proportions, preserves this elegance in the details, in the greater number and fineness of its mouldings, the more delicate and less sparingly distributed ornamentation. The Doric order seems to be designed for buildings of the largest size, or which, from their situation should be viewed from a distance; the Ionic seems more adapted to edifices intended for closer view, so as to engage the eyes by the delicacy of the details.

Eugène Viollet-le-Duc, 'Lectures on Architecture', 1858–72

Capital of a Greek Doric temple at Metaponto, Italy. 5th century BC

The first explorers of Chichén Itzá

And from this lofty height we saw for the first time groups of small columns, which, on examination, proved to be among the most remarkable and unintelligible remains we have yet met with. They stood in rows of three, four, and five abreast, many rows continuing in the same direction, when they changed and pursued another. They were very low, many of them only three feet high, while the highest were not more than six feet, and consisted of several pieces, like millstones. Many of them had fallen, and in some places they lie prostrate in rows, all in the same direction, as if thrown down intentionally. I had a large number of Indians at work clearing them, and endeavouring to trace their direction to the end ... They enclose an area nearly four hundred feet square; and incomprehensible as they are in their uses and object, add largely to the interest and wonder connected with these ruins.

John Lloyd Stephens, 'Incidents of Travel in Yucatan', 1841

70 Temple of Horus, Edfu, Egypt.
71 Remains of a colonnaded hall at Chichén Itzá, Yucatán, Mexico.
72 Rock-cut temples, Elephanta, near Bombay, India.
73 Angkor Thom, Cambodia.
74 Buddhist shrine in Cambodia.
75 The bull Nandi in the Hoysaleshwara Temple, Halebid, India.

Humanism

It is not at all improbable that they borrowed the proportions of their columns from that of the members of the human body. Thus they found that from one side of a man to the other was a sixth part of his height, and from the navel to the reins was a tenth. From this observation, the interpreters of our sacred books are of the opinion that Noah's ark for the flood was built upon the proportions of the human body. By the same proportions we may reasonably conjecture that the ancients erected their columns.

Leon Battista Alberti, 'De re aedificatoria', 1485

Palladian principle

An even number of columns ought always to be placed in the fronts of edifices, that an intercolumniation may be made in the middle somewhat larger than the others, that the doors and entries usually placed in the middle, may be the better seen.

Andrea Palladio 'Quattro Libri dell'Architettura', 1570

The primacy of the orders

The orders of architecture are the basis upon which the whole decorative part of the art is chiefly built and towards which the attention of the artist must ever be directed, even where no orders are introduced. In them originate most of the forms used in decoration; they regulate most of the proportions; and to their combination, multiplied, varied and arranged in a thousand different ways, architecture is indebted for its most splendid productions.

Sir William Chambers 'Treatise on Civil Architecture', 1759

The architect's alphabet

To the orders of architecture all buildings are indebted for the highest magnificence of decoration; to them the architect is obliged for many of the greatest effects in his art. The student must therefore be well acquainted with all the varieties in the work of the Ancients, and acquire the fullest knowledge and most clear and correct ideas of their constituent principles. They form, as it were, his alphabet and have indeed been by many considered as the standard of taste never to be altered.

76 Hieroglyphic writing at Medinet Habu, Egypt.

Sir John Soane, 'Lectures in Architecture', 1809–36

COLUMNS
THE CAPITAL AND THE BASE

THE TOP AND BOTTOM OF THE COLUMN are the key points where load meets support and support meets the ground. A large part of the history of architecture could be written in terms of the different ways these two points have been treated – how classical orders were modified in Byzantine, Gothic and Renaissance times, transformed almost out of recognition and then recovered and revived. The capital is that part of the column that is compressed under the load. It expands under pressure; it unfurls as a volute or hides itself behind foliage or figures. The base expresses strength and solidity as it merges with the earth.

The orders attained pre-eminence in almost all branches of western architecture after the Renaissance, and the exact and detailed specification of their various parts forms the largest single theme of architectural literature. Every work of criticism and every builders' manual up to the early twentieth century is bound to include it. To master the subject in all its subtlety and refinement needed long study, but there was little new to say, and the result cannot avoid a good deal of repetition.

Base of a column of the Hellenistic
Temple of Apollo at Didyma, Turkey

Saqqara

It is ... the most ancient building in the world. It had been standing from five to seven hundred years when King Cheops began his Great Pyramid at Geezeh. It was over two thousand years old when Abraham was born. It is now about six thousand eight hundred years old according to Manetho and Mariette, or about four thousand eight hundred according to the computation of Bunsen. One's imagination recoils upon the brink of such a gulf of time.

Amelia B. Edwards, 'A Thousand Miles up the Nile', 1877

82

84

Function expressed

In classical architecture, we speak of supporting and supported members. Many people, it is true, associate nothing in particular with this. But others receive the impression of a heavy burden weighing down the column, just as it would a human being. This is very literally illustrated where the supporting element has been given human form, such as a caryatid or an atlas – a petrified giant straining all his muscles under his load. The same conception is expressed in Greek columns by the slight outward curvature of profile, the *entasis*, which gives an impression of straining muscles – a surprising thing to find in a rigid and unresponsive pillar of stone.

Steen Eiler Rasmussen, 'Experiencing Architecture', 1959

Neo-classical rules

1st, a column ought to be exactly perpendicular, because being designed to support all the weight, it is the perfect line that gives it its strength. 2ndly, the column ought to be detached, to express more naturally its origins and design. 3rdly, the column should be round, as nature forms nothing square. 4thly, the column should have its diminution from the bottom to the top, as imitating nature which gives this sort of diminution to all plants. 5thly, a column should bear immediately upon the pavement, as the pillars of the rustic cabin bear immediately upon the ground.

Abbé Laugier, 'Essai sur l'Architecture', 1753

An English view of Corinthian

It is not surprising that it should have been the Corinthian, the last and flashiest of the three Greek orders, which the Romans used most frequently, nor that in their efforts to outdo the Greeks they should have been led to concentrate on an extreme richness of decoration, which must, one imagines, have, have rendered Rome in all its glory a trifle overpowering. Augustus, we are told, found the city brick and left it marble, but several of the recent charges in London do not encourage one to believe that such a metamorphosis was necessarily a change for the better.

Sir Osbert Lancaster, 'Pillar to Post', 1938

85   Vakil Mosque, Shiraz, Iran.

III ARCHES

A FLAT LINTEL expresses stability but not movement. The arch is alive, tracing the line of force and meeting it with an equal and opposite force. In the words of the old masonic proverb, 'the arch never sleeps'. Islamic architects adapted the arch, using it functionally, but even more as a means of articulating surfaces. In Gothic Europe, the arch became the basis of both the functional and the decorative parts of architecture. It reduced a building to a skeleton, allowing tracery and glass to fill the spaces in between. As the column, with its capital and base, tended to separate one element from another, the arch tended to unite them.

Architecture has always provided a potent symbolic image of the universe and man's apprehension of it. The philosopher Oswald Spengler defined whole cultures in terms of their architectures — the classical ('Euclidean') whose world is based on clearly perceived geometrical forms; the Islamic ('Magian') whose world-image is the cave; and the Gothic ('Faustian') where all the forms point 'upward and onward', away from the finite and towards the infinite.

Courtyard of the monastery of Rila, Bulgaria. 19th century

An 18th century traveller at Ephesus

The condition to which that renowned city has been gradually reduced. It was a ruinous place when the emperor Justinian filled Constantinople with its statues, and raised his church of St Sophia on its columns. Since then it has been almost quite exhausted. Its streets are obscured and overgrown. A herd of goats was driven to it for shelter from the sun at noon; and a noisy flight of crows from the quarries seemed to insult its silence. We heard the partridge call in the arc of the theatre and of the stadium. The glorious pomp of its heathen worship is no longer remembered; and Christianity, which was there nursed by apostles and fostered by general councils, until it increased to fullness of stature, barely lingers on in an existence hardly visible.

Richard Chandler, 'Travels in Asia Minor', 1775

86 Reconstructed façade of the temple erected by Hadrian at Ephesus, Turkey.
87 Roman amphitheatre at Arles, southern France.
88 Basilica of Maxentius, Rome.
89 Roman triumphal arch near St Rémy, southern France.
90 The Forum, Rome, with the Arch of Septimius Severus in the background.
91 Covered passage in the ruined palace of Ukheidir, Iraq.
92 Shell of the Blachernae Palace, Constantinople, Turkey.

A view of Ukheidir

It reared its mighty walls out of the sand, almost untouched by time, breaking the long lines of the waste with its huge towers, steadfast and massive, as though it were, as I had first thought, the work of nature, not of man.

Gertrude Bell, 'Amurath ro Amurath', 1911

S. Ambrogio, Milan

Entering at the west end it presents a most striking and, to me, most novel effect. In advance of the church is an open atrium, surrounded by a cloister of Lombard-Romanesque character, the columns having quaintly and stiffly carved capitals of stone, and the wall and arches being built of mixed brick and stone. Three arches open from the atrium to the west end of the church, and above them three other arches of similar plan and arranged in triplet fashion, that in the centre being the highest and widest, nearly fill up the great flat pediment of the church, on either side of which rise towers   that on the north divided into stages by means of arcaded strings, like most Lombard belfries; that on the south perfectly plain and rude.

G. E. Street, 'Brick and Marble in the Middle Ages', 1855

93   Atrium of the church of S. Ambrogio, Milan, Italy.

*Islamic arches on re-used
Roman columns in
a mosque in North Africa*

Monreale Cathedral

Every yard of its 70,000 square feet is covered with Byzantine mosaics completed in 1182. In the nave, subjects from the Old Testament: in the aisles and transepts scenes from the Life of Christ. On the arches of the transept are scenes from the lives of SS. Peter and Paul, while in the Tribune we see the vast bust of Christ with an inscription in Greek and below the Madonna and Child enthroned with angels and saints and below again the Apostles. The spaces over the arch dividing the sanctuary from the minor tribune are adorned with figures of twelve prophets. An arch leading from the minor tribune into the transept is decorated with a half figure of Christ and eight medallions of prophets. On the other face of the arch is the Annunciation. In the archivaults in the centre of the church we see medallions of the progenitors of Christ. And over the arch dividing this vault from the nave is S. Sofia the Divine Wisdom of God, adored by the archangels S. Michael and S. Gabriel.

Edward Hutton, 'Cities of Sicily', 1926

94   Mosaics above the arcade of Monreale
      Cathedral, Sicily.
95   Cathedral of Gerace, southern Italy.
96   S. Stefano Rotondo, Rome.
97   Substructure of arches, part of the remains of
      Roman Izmir (Smyrna), Turkey.
98   The bridge of Avignon, France.
99   Basilica of Aquileia, Italy.
100   Crumbling walls and arches of Hierapolis,
      Turkey.
101   Bridge across the stagnant moat that surrounds
      the medieval castle of Tarascon, in the south
      of France.

97

98

The three ages of the arch

Consider, again, the beautiful notion of uniting the round arch and the column; this again is a Syrian, if not a north-Arabian creation of the third (or 'high Gothic') century. The revolutionary importance of this motive, which is specifically Magian, has never in the least degree been realized; on the contrary, it has always been assumed to be Classical, and for most of us indeed it is representatively Classical. The Egyptians did not see any deep relation between the roof and the column; the latter was for them a plant-column, and represented not stoutness but growth. Classical man, in his turn, for whom the monolithic column was the mightiest symbol of Euclidean existence – all body, all unity, all steadiness – connected it, in the strictest proportions of vertical and horizontal, of strength and load, with its architrave. But here, in this union of arch and column which the Renaissance in its tragicomic deludedness admired as expressly Classical (though it was a notion that the Classical neither possessed nor could possess), the bodily principle of load and inertia is rejected and the arch is made to spring clear and open out of the slender column. The idea actualized here is at once a liberation from all earth-gravity and a capture of space, and between this element and that of the dome which soars free but yet encloses the great 'cavern' there is the deep relation of like meaning. The one and the other are eminently and powerfully Magian, and they come to their logical fulfilment in the 'Rococo' stage of Moorish mosques and castles, wherein etherially delicate columns – often growing out of rather than based on the ground – seem to be empowered by some secret magic to carry a whole world of innumerable notched arcs, gleaming ornaments, stalactites and vaultings saturated with colours. The full importance of this basic form of Arabian architecture may be expressed by saying that the combination of pillar and architrave is the Classical, that of column and round arch the Arabian, and that of pillar and pointed arch the Faustian Leitomtif.

Oswald Spengler, 'The Decline of the West', 1918

102   Valle Crucis Abbey, Wales.

IV AQUEDUCTS & BRIDGES

There is hardly any aspect of architecture that has not been, and is not still, given vitality by the use of the arch. Single, it is the triumphal arch, a building type which came to be the *leitmotiv* of the Roman Empire, embodying both its achievement and its brutal pride. Prolonged into a series of arches, an arcade, it was the favourite method of articulating the exterior of classical buildings. The most famous example is the Coliseum, the progeny of which can be seen throughout history in every sort of architecture from palaces to railway stations. The Christian church, by a seemingly inevitable choice, made it the dominant feature of its interiors, raising one arcade upon another in the majestic sequence of aisle, gallery and clerestory; (just how *un*inevitable it was is clear from the fact that no other religious buildings in the world use it).

Given such ancestry and such associations, it is not surprising therefore, that when sequences of arches are employed for purely utilitarian purposes they should have such an effect of grandeur. Bridges and aqueducts are among the most moving of structures for their form only. Often designed by engineers with no thought beyond the strength of materials and the mathematics of stress, they become works of art through the abstract beauty of their geometry.

Roman aqueduct at Segovia, Spain

A Renaissance visitor to Tivoli

About three miles from Tivoli the Emperor Hadrian built a magnificent villa like a big town. Lofty vaults of great temples still stand and the half-ruined structures of halls and chambers are to be seen. There are also remains of peristyles and huge columned porticoes and swimming pools and baths, into which part of the Aniene was once turned to cool the summer heat. Time has marred everything. The walls once covered with embroidered tapestries and hangings threaded with gold are now clothed with ivy. Briers and brambles have sprung up where purple-robed tribunes sat and queens' chambers are the lairs of serpents. So fleeting are mortal things!

Aeneas Sylvius Piccolomini
(Pope Pius II), 'Commentaries', 1464

107

108

III

114

115

116

117

V DOMES
THE EXTERIOR

THE DOME is one of the most primitive as well as one of the most sophisticated of architectural forms. A cairn of stones is domical. Funeral monuments, gigantic cairns, often assumed a domical shape, of which Roman mausolea are the developed examples. In Asia the stupa was in origin a funerary mound which came also to function as an image of the universe.

The Pantheon is a large dome based on the ground. Byzantine architects seem to have been the first to conceive the idea of building domes in the air. That of Hagia Sophia, in Constantinople, was first and remains for many the most beautiful. Its shape is that of a shallow 'saucer' dome. Gothic architects ventured on small octagonal domes over the crossings of cathedrals. It was Brunelleschi, at Florence, who dared to build such a dome on an enormous scale. Michelangelo, at St Peter's, made his circular, in emulation of the Pantheon, and during the seventeenth and eighteenth centuries it was the most ambitious form to which architecture could aspire.

Hagia Sophia, Istanbul. 6th century

Ruskin on the domes of St. Mark's

Domes are native to the east, where they concentrate light upon their orbed surfaces and where the bulging form may also be delightful, from the idea of its enclosing a volume of cool air. Their chief charm is, to the European eye, that of strangeness. I enjoy them at St. Mark's chiefly because they increase the fantastic and unreal character of St. Mark's Place; and because they appear to sympathize with an expression of natural buoyancy, as if they floated in the air or on the surface of the sea.

John Ruskin, Notes for 'The Stones of Venice', 1846

127

The placing of domes

The domes of the ancients seem always to grow out of the substructure and to harmonize and unite with it in the most gradual and pleasing manner, forming as it were a canopy to the entire edifice. In many modern structures, domes seem to be placed on the roofs without any visible support, and without any apparent connection with the other parts of the edifice. It must likewise be remarked that modern domes, instead of being terminated with light and appropriate ornaments, as in ancient works, are now often surcharged with lanterns of very large considerable dimensions, both in bulk and height. However general this fashion may be, it is not less deserving of censure, for as the dome represents the roof of a square, polygonal or circular building, how can we add a lantern, or any other building, to a dome?

Sir John Soane, 'Lectures in Architecture', 1809–36

Nec plus ultra

To judge by the inventiveness shown and the widespread use of domes in modern time, by the prodigious expense that they involve, and the efforts of every sort that they require, by the spirit of emulation that has led all the peoples of Europe to challenge each other in this way in daring, scale and magnificence and by the admiration and critical attention that is everywhere lavished upon them, it is tempting to believe that this achievement constitutes the peak of architectural ambition, that it alone was lacking to the glory of the ancients, and that finally the dome unites all that is most beautiful in all beautiful works, to become the *nec plus ultra* of science and of art.

Quatremère de Quincy, 'Dictionnaire historique d'Architecture', 1832

In the poet's eye

There massie Columns in a Circle rise,
O'er which a pompous Dome invades the Skies,
Scarce to the Top I stretched my aching Sight,
So large it spread, and swelled to such a Height.

Alexander Pope, 'The Temple of Fame', 1712

132   Dome of Florence Cathedral, Italy.

DOMES
THE INTERIOR

IF THE DOME from outside represents the earth, from inside it represents the sky. In ancient times the sky was naturally seen as the 'vault' of the earth, and by analogy the ceilings of houses and sacred buildings have been decorated with stars, an effect made even more vivid when the shape was hemispherical. In the twentieth century this idea reached its logical conclusion with the invention of of the planetarium.

There is a great deal of architectural writing about domes and vaults, but it is mostly of a severely technical nature. Throughout history, the covering of large spaces by unsupported spans has posed the greatest of engineering challenges, and has often been held to be the determining factor in architectural progress. It is certainly true that our awareness of internal space depends almost entirely on the system by which the roof is supported. The history of space is the history of architecture.

Interior of the Pantheon, Rome. 2nd century AD

In here is a cupola which by its height becomes lost from sight; beauty in it appears both concealed and visible.

The constellation of Gemini extends a ready hand [to help it] and the full moon of the heavens draws near to whisper secretly to it.

And the bright stars would like to establish themselves firmly in it rather than to continue wandering about in the vault of the sky.

Were they to remain in its antechambers they would outstrip the handmaidens in serving you in such a way as to cause you to be pleased with them.

It is no wonder that it surpasses the stars in the heavens, and passes beyond their furthest limits.

For it is before your dwelling that it has arisen to perform its service, since he who serves the highest acquires merits thereby.

Part of an Arabic inscription in the Sala de las Dos Hermanas, Alhambra, Granada

141

142

A new awareness

When and where the various possibilities of dome, cupola, barrel-vaulting and rib-vaulting came into existence as technical methods is a matter of no significance. What is of decisive importance is the fact that about the time of Christ's birth and the rise of the new-world feeling, the new space-symbolism must have begun to make use of these forms and to develop them further in expressiveness.

Oswald Spengler, 'The Decline of the West', 1918

Hadrian dedicates the Pantheon

My intention has been that this sanctuary of All Gods should reproduce the likeness of the terrestrial globe and the stellar sphere, that globe wherein are enclosed the seeds of eternal time, and that hollow sphere containing all. Such was also the form of our ancestors' huts where the smoke of man's earliest hearths escaped through an orifice at the top. The cupola, constructed of hard but light-weight volcanic stone, which seemed still to share in the upward movement of flames, revealed the sky through a great hole at the centre showing alternately dark and blue. This temple, both open and mysteriously enclosed, was conceived as a solar quadrant. The hours would make their round on that caissoned ceiling, so carefully polished by Greek artisans; the disk of daylight would rest suspended there like a shield of gold; rain would form its clear pool on the pavement below; prayers would rise like smoke toward that void where we place the gods.

*The Emperor Hadrian, as imagined by Marguerite Yourcenar
in 'Memoirs of Hadrian', 1952*

The Greek cosmos

When Propertius describes the temple of Zeus at Olympia as 'imitating the sky' he is in all probability alluding to the coffered ceiling with its gilt stars on a blue ground – a device common to Greek with Egyptian art. The same conception of the pillared sky found ritual expression in the great festival tent erected by Ion at Delphi. That this was an imitation of the sky is clear, not only from the fact that it was made big enough to hold the entire populace, but also from the cosmic decoration of the roof.

A. B. Cook, 'Zeus', 1914–40

149 Chancel of Cuenca Cathedral, Spain.

VI CEILINGS

FROM THE CONCEPT OF THE VAULT AS SKY grew the practice, from the Renaissance onwards, of decorating ceilings with *trompe-l'oeil* paintings where the spectator, gazing upwards, saw angels floating in space or the heavens opening for saints to ascend or Christ to come down in judgment. The artists of the Baroque, with their sense of theatre and their mastery of perspective, could bring the whole decor of a church into a unified scheme to create a single illusionistic experience – though always with the proviso that the viewer had to stand in exactly the right spot for the illusion to work.

The painted ceiling in a sense denied the architecture of the building, and was for this reason, one suspects, never completely accepted by architects. The alternative was to stress the solidity of the covering and its unity with the structure. In Gothic architecture this had been achieved by the rib vaults that sprang directly from the wall-shafts. Neo-classical designers evolved a decorative language in which ceiling patterns reflected or subtly varied those of the floor.

203

Church of Sant' Agnese fuori le mura, Rome; Renaissance ceiling on an Early Christian church

A Protestant view of Baroque

Amid the many distinguished men whom the Jesuits sent forth to every region of the world, I cannot recollect the name of a single artist, unless it be the Father Pozzi, renowned for his skill in perspective, and who used his skill less as an artist than a conjurer, to produce such illusions as make the vulgar stare; — to make the impalpable to the grasp appear as palpable to the vision; the near seem distant, the distant near; the unreal, real; to cheat the eye; to dazzle the sense; — all this has Father Pozzi most cunningly achieved in the Gesù and the Sant' Ignazio at Rome; but nothing more, and nothing better than this. I wearied of his altar-pieces and of his wonderful roofs which pretend to be no roofs at all. Scheme, tricks, and deceptions in art should all be kept for the theatre. It appeared to me nothing less than profane to introduce *shams* into the temples of God.

Mrs Anna Jameson, 'Legends of the Monastic Orders', 1850

150   Vault of one of the *iwans* of the Friday Mosque, Isfahan, Iran.

151   Fallen ceiling panels from the Hoysaleshwara Temple, Halebid, India.

152   Vault of S. Giovanni Evangelista, Parma, Italy.

153   Roof of Orvieto Cathedral, Italy.

154   Ceiling of the Camera degli Sposi in the Ducal Palace, Mantua, Italy.

155   *Sala terrena* of the Villa Cicogna, Bisuschio, Italy.

150

155

ET QVID VOLO NISI

VT ACCENDATVR

The Gothic forest

If you entered the interior of a medieval cathedral, it did not represent to me the strength and mechanical efficiency of the carrying piers and of the vaulting resting upon them, but rather a forest vault, whose ranks of trees incline their branches towards each other and intertwine.

G. W. F. Hegel, 'Aesthetic', 1840

Roof-structures

Whether of timber or stone, roofs are necessarily divided into surfaces and ribs or beams; – surfaces flat or curved; ribs traversing these in the directions where main strength is required; or beams filling the hollow of the dark gable with the intricate roof-tree, or supporting the flat ceiling . . . I have never myself seen a flat ceiling satisfactorily decorated, except by painting.

John Ruskin, 'The Stones of Venice', 1851

The crowning proportions

Ceilings are also diversely made, because many take delight to have them of beautiful and well-wrought beams. It is necessary to observe that these beams ought to be distant from one another one thickness and a half of the beam. The ceilings appears thus very beautiful to the eye, and there remains so much of the wall between the ends of the beams that it is more able to sustain what is over it.

Andrea Palladio, 'Quattro Libri dell'Architettura', 1570

On Adam-style ceilings

Painted ceilings, which constitute one of the great embellishments of Italian and French structures, and in which the greatest masters have displayed their utmost abilities, are not in use among us. For one cannot suffer to go by so high a name, the trifling, gaudy ceilings now in fashion, which, composed as they are of little rounds, squares, octagons, hexagons and ovals, excite no other idea than that of a dessert, upon the plates of which are dished out bad copies of indifferent antiques. They certainly have neither fancy, taste, splendour, execution, nor any other striking quality to recommend them.

Sir William Chambers, 'Treatise on Civil Architecture', 1759

156 Detail of the ceiling of S. Ignazio, Rome.

VII ROOFS

THE ROOF is the most utilitarian part of a building, the part where efficiency is essential at whatever cost to beauty. It has, moreover, to be seen from a peculiar perspective, and can only be properly appreciated from a distance. Classical architects solved the problem by ignoring it: their roofs are either flat or discretely hidden behind parapets (a strategy endorsed by Sir Christopher Wren).

Outside the areas of classical influence, however, the roof often assumed a major role in design. The skyline of Northern Europe during the Middle Ages and up to the seventeenth century must have been fascinating for its display of roofs. The determining factor – as noted by many of the writers on the subject – was weather. In roofs, more than in any other part of the building, climatic variations produced architectural variety.

Model Japanese pagoda

The legend of S. Teodoro, Rome

It is curious to note in Rome how many a modern superstition has its root in an ancient one, and how tenaciously customs still cling to the old localities. On the Capitoline hill the bronze she-wolf was once worshipped as the wooden Bambino is now. It stood in the Temple of Romulus, and there the ancient Romans used to carry children to be cured of their diseases by touching it. On the supposed site of the temple now stands the church dedicated to S. Teodoro, or Santo Toto, as he is called in Rome. Though names must have changed and the temple has vanished, and church after church has here decayed and been rebuilt, the old superstition remains, and the common people at certain periods still bring their sick children to Santo Toto, that he may heal them with his touch.

William Wetmore Story, 'Roba di Roma', 1863

157

158

159

163

164

Flat roofs preferred

No roof can have dignity enough to appear above a cornice but the circular: in private buildings it is excusable. The Ancients affected flatness.

Sir Christopher Wren, 'Parentalia', before 1723

Sloping roofs advised

For rain is always prepared to do mischief, and wherever there is the least crack never fails to get in and do some hurt or other. By its subtlety it penetrates and makes its way, by its humidity it rots and destroys, by its continuance loosens and unknits all the nerves of the buildings, and in the end ruins and lays waste the whole structure to the very foundations. And for this reason prudent architects have always taken care that the rain should have a free slope to run off, and that the water should never be stopped in any place where it could do hurt. And therefore they advised that in places subject to much snow, the coverings should have a very steep slope, rising even to a very acute angle, that the snow might never rest and gather upon them, but fall off easily.

Leon Battista Alberti, 'De re aedificatoria', 1485

Silhouettes

It is a mistaken idea to consider roofs as mere matters of convenience and utility. Roofs on the contrary assist materially in embellishing or destroying the general effect of the whole building. The greater the opposition and contrast in their forms, in buildings of considerable extent, the greater and more pleasing will be the effect, not only of the roofing but of the whole external appearance.

Sir John Soane, 'Lectures on Architecture', 1809–36

Domestic embellishment

The high roofs of pointed domestic architecture, though subjects which admitted of little ornament, were not left without relief by our old builders. This relief they derived variously from the use of numerous lead rolls, when lead was the covering; or in other cases from the employment of shingles or wooden tiles of different shapes, producing a pleasing alternation of line; besides which, there are instances of a finishing for the ridges of roofs, formed of what were called crest-tiles, a little ornament of open work bearing an application very analogous to that of the ridge tiles of a Greek temple.

J. C. Loudon, 'Encyclopaedia of Cottage, Farm and Villa Architecture', 1836

166   Golden Pavilion, Kyoto, Japan.

VIII STAIRCASES

OF ALL THE ELEMENTS of architecture, a staircase is the least capable of being appreciated as a complete whole. It can only be experienced sequentially. This gives the architect a unique opportunity to determine the sensations of the spectator at each point, almost like the stage manager of a theatre. He must also think simultaneously in two dimensions of time, for people go both up and down a staircase: it must work in both directions. A staircase is like a path, of which the destination can be openly displayed or concealed; the means of approach can be grandiose or intimate; it can lead forward irresistibly or it can detain with a thousand distractions.

There are exciting staircases in reality; even more exciting ones in fantasy. The most haunting of all is that which appears in De Quincey's account of Piranesi's prison etchings. De Quincey had never seen these etchings, and in fact misdescribes them, but he understood them intuitively because they chimed with his experiences under opium (see p. 237). Compared with this extraordinary vision the writings on staircases by architects themselves seem humdrum. It was a subject that preoccupied them because of its practical problems. But what is interesting is that from such utilitarian aims should spring such marvellously imaginative results.

Staircase in Laval University, Quebec, Canada. 19th century

The Theatre of Epidauros

The Epidaurians have a theatre in their sanctuary that seems to me particularly worth a visit. The Roman theatres have gone far beyond all others in the whole world: the theatre of Magalopolis in Arkadia is unique for magnitude. But who can begin to rival Polykleitos for the beauty or composition of his architecture? It was Polykleitos who built the theatre and the round building.

Pausanias, 'Guide to Greece', 2nd century AD

167 Path at Cumae, Italy.
168 Theatre of Palmyra, Syria.
169 Theatre of Epidauros, Greece.
170 Temple of Apollo, Didyma, Turkey.
171 Great Staircase, Persepolis, Iran.

De Quincey on Piranesi's etchings

Some of them represented vast Gothic halls on the floor of which stood all sorts of engines and machinery, wheels, cables, pulleys, levers, catapults, &c. &c., expressive of enormous power put forth and resistance overcome. Creeping along the sides of the walls you perceived a staircase; and upon it, groping his way upwards, was Piranesi himself: follow the stairs a little further and you perceive it come to a sudden and abrupt termination without any balustrade, and allowing no step onwards to him who had reached the extremity except into the depths below. Whatever is to become of poor Piranesi, you suppose at least that his labours must in some way terminate here. But raise your eyes, and behold a second flight of stairs still higher, on which again Piranesi is perceived, but this time standing on the very brink of the abyss. Again elevate your eye, and a still more aerial flight of stairs is beheld, and again is poor Piranesi busy on his aspiring labours; and so on, until the unfinished stairs and Piranesi both are lost in the upper gloom of the hall. With the same power of endless growth and self-reproduction did my architecture proceed in dreams. In the early stage of my malady the splendours of my dreams were indeed chiefly architectural; and I beheld such pomp of cities and palaces as was never yet beheld by the waking eye unless in the clouds.

Thomas De Quincey, 'Confessions of an English Opium Eater', 1822

The staircase in Antiquity

If we examine the dimensions of the steps leading into the peristyles of ancient temples, they will be found to be proportioned to the ordonnance, magnitude and character of the building rather than for ease of ascent. Indeed, we cannot expect to gain much information on this head from the ancients, when it is considered that their buildings, in general, both public and private, consisted of a ground floor only. Staircases are mentioned by Homer, and Lysias in one of his Orations speaks of two storeys, while at Pompeii there is an instance of a house with a second floor; but as Pliny and Varro do not mention staircases in the description of their villas, it is reasonable to conclude that they were of very inconsiderable extent. In modern works, both public and private, staircases are the very touchstone of sound knowledge and real merit in the architect. In every building they are features of such importance that to determine their proper situation, character and extent, as well as their most suitable forms and proper decorations, requires all the experience and judgement of the most able architects.

172   Staircase of the citadel of Yapahuwa, Sri Lanka.

Sir John Soane, 'Lectures on Architecture', 1809–36

Stairs in the design

The placing of the stairs is a work of such nicety, that without deliberate and mature consideration you can never place them well. For a staircase there must be three apertures: one, the door by which you enter upon the stairs; another, the window which supplies you with light to see the steps by; and the third, the opening in the ceiling which lets you into the area above. And therefore it is said to be no wonder that the stairs should perplex the design of a structure; but let him that is desirous to have the stair not hinder him, take care not to hinder the stair, but allow it a determinate and just portion of the platform, in order to give it free course quite up to the covering at the top of all.

Leon Battista Alberti, 'De re aedificatoria', 1485

Feet on the stairs

To make a complete staircase is a curious piece of architecture. The vulgar cautions are these. That it may have a very liberal light, against all casualty of slips and falls. That the space above the head be large and airy, which the Italians used to call *un bel sfogolo*, as it were good ventilation, because a man doth spend much breath in mounting. That the half-paces be well distributed, at competent distances, for reposing on the way. That to avoid encounters and besides to gratify the beholder, the whole staircase have no nigard latitude, that is for the principal ascent, at least ten foot in royal buildings. That the breadth of every single step or stair be never less than one foot, nor more than eighteen inches. That they exceed by no means half a foot in their height or thickness; for our legs do labour more in elevation than in distention. These, I say, are familiar remembrances, to which let me add: that the steps be laid where they join *con un tantino di scarpa*. We may translate it 'somewhat sloping', so that the foot may in a sort both ascend and descend together, which though observed by a few, is a secret and delicate deception of the pains of mounting.

Sir Henry Wotton, 'The Elements of Architecture', 1624

Palladio's advice

Great care ought to be taken in the placing of staircases, because it is no small difficulty to find a situation fit for them, and that doth not impede the remaining part of the fabric. A proper place must therefore be principally given them, that they may not obstruct other places, nor be obstructed by them.

The staircases will be commendable if they are clear, ample, and commodious to ascend, inviting, as it were, people to go up. They will be clear, if they have a bright light, and if the light be diffused equally everywhere alike. They will be sufficiently ample, if they do not seem scanty and narrow to the largeness and quality of the fabric; but they are never to be made less wide than two foot, that if two persons meet they may conveniently give one another room. They will be convenient with respect to the whole building, if the arches under them can serve to lodge some necessaries; and with respect to men, if their ascent is not too steep and difficult; therefore their length must be twice their height.

The ancients observed to make the steps uneven in number that beginning to go up with the right foot, one might end with the same; which they looked upon as a good omen, and of greater devotion when they entered the temple. The number of steps is not to exceed eleven, or thirteen at most, before you make a floor or meeting place, that the weak and weary may find where to rest themselves, if obliged to go up higher.

Staircases are either made straight or winding; the straight are either made to spread into two branches or square which turn into four branches. To make these the whole place is to be divided into four parts; two are given to the steps and two to the void in the middle, from which these stairs would have light, if it was left uncovered.

The winding staircases are in some places made round, in others oval, sometimes with a column in the middle, and sometimes void, in narrow places particularly because they occupy less room than the straight, but are somewhat more difficult to ascend. They succeed very well that are void in the middle because they have the light from above, and those that are at the top of the stairs see all those that come up, or begin to ascend, and are likewise seen by them.

Andrea Palladio, 'Quattro Libri dell'Architettura', 1570

Dickens at the Palazzo Ducale

Descending from the palace by a staircase, called, I thought, the Giant's, I had some imaginary recollection of an old man abdicating, coming more slowly and more feebly down it, when he heard the bell, proclaiming his successor'.

Charles Dickens, 'Pictures from Italy', 1846

177

178

In palaces

In a palace, it is best to carry the grand staircase up no higher than one storey. There may indeed be several more storeys above it – to provide rooms for servants and private apartments for the family – but these may be reached by smaller staircases which lead eventually to the attics and the roof. The grand staircase should lead nowhere but to the first storey. In this way its form can be most fruitfully developed, and its ceiling, which often consists of a shallow dome or a vault with an entablature decorated with sculptures, etc, can be best appreciated.

Quatremère de Quincy, 'Dictionnaire historique d'Architecture', 1832

At the top of the stairs

With respect to the winding stairs, regarded as a relic of the 'toys' of the Middle Ages, I remark that they are very useful toys when we wish to contrive a way to the upper storeys in a small space. Might we not with more reason give the name of 'great toys' to those double flights of stairs which take up unnecessary room in our buildings, and which by their exaggerated monumental character, always remind one of those preambles of the poets, announcing in pompous strains the fine things that never come.

Eugène Viollet-le-Duc, 'Lectures on Architecture', 1858–72

180   Outside the Yeni Valide Mosque, in Istanbul, Turkey.

IX FLOORS AND PAVEMENTS

As THE VAULT represents the sky, so the floor represents the ground or the level surface of the sea. But of all the elements of architecture, the floor is the least designed for display, since it must always be concealed either by covering of some sort or by furniture. Indeed, the Romans made their floors imitate carpets, or used them to tell stories in mosaic. At Ostia, the pavements outside shops announced the wares that were for sale within.

Paradoxically, ancient architecture survives largely in its floors, when every other element has disappeared. There are a thousand classical floors for every classical roof. Add to these the paved roads of ruined cities, often touchingly intact when the thresholds to which they lead have been tenantless for millennia.

Roman floor mosaic at Caeseria
(Cherchell), Algeria

Farewell to the Via Sacra

For the last time I mounted the Capitol, which rose like a fairy palace in the desert ... Sombre itself, and throwing sombre shades, stood the triumphal arch of Septimius Severus. In the solitude of the Via Sacra the objects, otherwise so well known, appeared foreign and ghost-like. As, however, I approached the sublime remains of the Coliseum, and looked through the grating into its closed interior, a shudder came over me which, I do not deny, quickened my return.

Goethe, 'Travels in Italy', 1787

Choices of floor

Pavements are usually made either of terrazzo, as is used in Venice, bricks or live stones. Those terrazzi are excellent that are made of pounded bricks and small gravel and lime of river pebbles; and ought to be made in spring or in summer, that they may be well dried. Brick floors, because the bricks may be made of diverse forms and of diverse colours by reason of the diversity of the chalks, will be very agreeable and beautiful to the eye. Those of live stone are very seldom made in chambers because they are exceedingly cold in winter; but they do very well in loggias and public places.

Andrea Palladio, 'Quattro Libri dell'Architettura', 1570

Earth's floor

The characteristic of a floor is its levelness, and possibly it is because water is the most level thing in nature that we seem to find evidence of a tendency to represent water on pavements.

W. R. Lethaby, 'Architecture, Nature and Magic', 1956

The limits of innovation

The decorator deals with three surfaces, those of ceiling, of walls and of floor. Of these the first two can be curved or flat. I do not think that even the most modern designer has yet made a curved floor.

H. S. Goodhart-Rendel, 'Vitruvian Nights', 1932

Permanent ways

Pavements delight in damp and wet air while they are making and endure best and longest in moist and shady places; and their chief enemies are the looseness of the earth and sudden droughts. For as repeated rains make the ground close and firm, so pavements, being heartily wetted, grow compact and hard as iron. That part of the pavement which is to receive the water falling from the gutters ought to be made of the largest and soundest stones, such as will not easily be worn away by the continued malice (if we may so call it) of the spouts that fall upon it.

Leon Battista Alberti, 'De re aedificatoria', 1485

187   Tomb of Shaikh Salim Chishti, Fatehpur Sikri, India.

X TOWERS, SPIRES AND CASTLES

TOWERS STAND for two things: aspiration and security. The first is the reason why they are associated with religious buildings, a fact which applies to virtually all faiths. Buddhist pagodas represent heaven; from the minarets of Islam the muezzin calls to prayer; and all over medieval Christendom towers dominated the landscape proclaiming the glory of God. The tower as secure refuge is the castle. What arose as the most practical of building types was also from the beginning seen as a symbol. No figure of speech is more universal than that of the safe stronghold from the enemy, the siege of goodness by the forces of evil.

There are endless towers and castles in literature, and it would be rewarding to trace how they are used and what they represent. The last two quotations in this anthology are taken from fiction, one from a time when castles were still a reality, even a threat, the other from the Romantic age when they had become thrilling evocations of a picturesque past. The historical associations of buildings and of styles are a matter not only of literary but also of architectural history. Would the Gothic revival have happened without the Gothic novel?

Tower of the Palazzo Vecchio,
Florence. 14th century

Milan cathedral : a critical view

Its architect appears to me to have been shocked at the necessity under which he lay of sacrificing the steep lines of roof so dear to him in his native land, and to have striven with all his might to provide a substitute for their vertical effect by the vertical lines of his panelled buttresses and walls, by the gabled outline of his parapets, and by the removal of such a mark of horizontalism as the commencement of the traceries of his windows even on one line. And his work is a most remarkable standing proof of the failure of such an attempt.

G. E. Street, 'Brick and Marble in the Middle Ages', 1855

188   Phoenician obelisks at Byblos, Lebanon.
189   Tower of S. Apollinare in Classe, Ravenna.
190   Pozzo di S. Patrizio, Orvieto, Italy.
191   Tower of S. Maria in Cosmedin, Rome.
192   Campanile and dome of Siena Cathedral, Italy.
193   Crossing tower of Milan Cathedral, Italy.
194   Church of Nuestra Señora del Pilar, Saragossa, Spain.
195   Crossing tower of Burgos Cathedral, Spain.

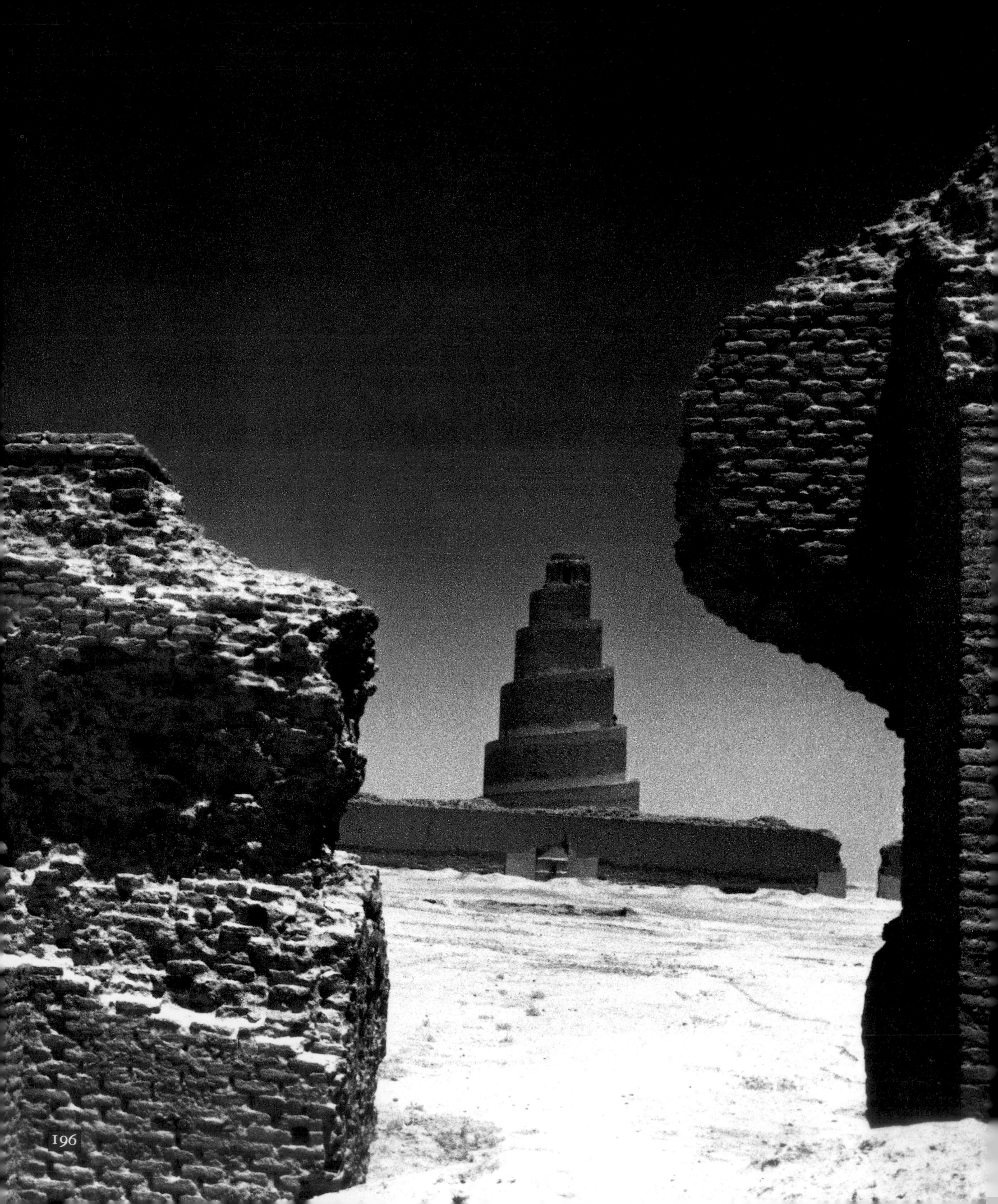

The cosmic tower

Ladder and palace coalesce in the stepped tower or ziggurat of the Babylonians, as in the *columna cochlis* of the Romans, to which the spiral tower of Samarra – a direct derivative of the ziggurat – bears a marked resemblance. The seven steps of the ziggurat – eight if we reckon, as Herodotus does, the sanctuary on the summit – have undoubtedly a cosmic significance, and correspond with the seven or eight steps of the Mithraic ladder or for that matter with the Sabian ladder of the seven planets.

A. B. Cook, 'Zeus', 1914–40

Abode of the gods

A jewelled pagoda of portentous dimensions is supposed, in the Buddhist cosmos, to tower upwards from the central peak of the sacred Mount Meru, to pierce the loftiest heaven and to illuminate the boundless ether with effulgent rays proceeding from the three jewels of the law and the revolving wheel with which it is crowned. Speculative symbolism of this kind is carried out in the form of the pagoda. The base, four-sided, represents the abode of the four maharajas, the great guardian kings of the four quarters, whose figures are seen enthroned representing the Tushita heaven, with eight celestial gods, Indra, Agni and the rest standing outside as protectors of the eight points of the compass; this is the paradise of the Buddhists prior to their final descent to the human world. The upper storey, circular in form, represents the highest heaven in which the Buddhas reside after attaining complete enlightenment.

S. W. Bushell, Chinese Art, 1904

Obelisks and spires

It is not improbable that the obelisks of Egypt suggested the idea of spires, and whatever partakes as distinctly of the pyramidal form may be reasonably supposed to refer to the worship of the sun. When spires unite and make a part of the building they accompany, they are entitled to all the praise that such fanciful compositions can claim; but where, instead of rising as it were, from the ground, they spring from apparent bases on the pediments of porticoes, no elegance of form, no variety of outline, can make such compositions at all bearable.

Sir John Soane, 'Lectures on Architecture', 1809–32

196   Minaret of the mosque at Samarra, Iraq.

Prospect towers are very desirable edifices in every country seat, and even in the grounds of suburban villas. Their use is to show a stranger the beauties of the surrounding scenery, and to admit of the occupant of the villa inspecting the appearance of his neighbourhood at different seasons of the year.

J. C. Loudon, 'Encyclopaedia of Cottage, Farm and Villa Architecture', 1836

Visionary towers

There might you see the lengthening Spires ascend,
The Domes swell up, the widening Arches bend,
The growing Towers like Exhalations rise,
And the huge Columns heave into the Skies.

Alexander Pope, 'The Temple of Fame', 1712

Pointers to Heaven

What indeed is more appropriate for the ancient worship than an old English parish church with its heaven-pointing spire – the beautiful and instructive emblem of a Christian's brightest hopes – with its solemn sounding bells to summon the people to the offices of the church, or to serve by their lofty elevation in the belfry towers as beacons to direct their footsteps to the sacred spot?

*A. W. N. Pugin, 'The True Principles of Pointed
or Christian Architecture', 1841*

The ultimate aspiration

And they said, Go to, let us build us a city and a tower whose top may reach unto heaven; and let us make us a name, lest we be scattered abroad upon the face of the whole earth. And the Lord came down to see the city and the tower which the children of men builded. And the Lord said, Behold, the people is one, and they have all one language, and this they begin to do; and now nothing will be restrained from them, which they have imagined to do.

Genesis XI

275

*Castello Scaligero, Sirmione, Italy.
13th century*

Architectural Surrealism

The church of la Sagrada Familia is not less peculiar that the most extreme works of Dalí or Picasso, more particularly when it is realized that it was begun as long ago as 1881, the year in which the latter painter was born. The architect Gaudí must be allowed talent or genius of an original order which could only be Spanish, and at that, Catalan, out of the whole of Spain. He guessed or anticipated the Art Nouveau, and then, at a longer hazard, Surrealism.

Sacheverell Sitwell, 'Spain', 1950

Italian townscape

The greatest ornaments are lofty towers placed in proper situations and built after handsome designs, and when there are a good number of them strewed up and down the country, they afford a most beautiful prospect. Not that I commend the age about two hundred years ago, when people seemed to be seized with a sort of general infection of building high watch-towers, even in the meanest villages, insomuch that scarce a common house-keeper thought he could be without his turret; by which means there arose a perfect grove of spires . . . Towers are either square or round, and in both these the height must answer in a certain proportion to the breadth. When they are designed to be very taper, square ones should be six times as high as they are broad and round ones should have four times the height of their diameter.

Leon Battista Alberti, 'De re aedificatoria', 1485

A safe stronghold

In the Middle Ages, towers became the principal, and almost the only, object of the art of architecture. Every palace was a stronghold, and the tradition of ancient fortification not having undergone any change, they built their houses following the ancient methods of attacking and defending towns. A château was nothing more than an assembly of towers, round or square, linked together by stretches of crenellated wall. This arrangement became universal and was applied to all types of building.

Quatremère de Quincy, 'Dictionnaire historique d'Architecture', 1832

A medieval picture

There were fair turrets fashioned between, with many loopholes well devised to shut fast. Gawain had never seen a better barbican. Further in he saw the hall rising high, with towers all about, whose pinnacles rose high aloft, with carven tops cunningly wrought. On the tower roofs his eye picked out many white chimneys that gleamed like chalk cliffs in the sunlight. And there were so many pinnacles, gaily painted, scattered about everywhere and climbing one above another among the embrasures of the castle, that it looked as though it were cut out of paper.

203 Rifai Mosque seen from the Mosque of Sultan Hassan, Cairo, Egypt.

'Sir Gawain and the Green Knight', late 14th century

Castel S. Angelo, Rome. The mausoleum of Hadrian converted into a fortress in medieval times

The building of Rumeli Hisar

Once back at Adrianople, Mehmet ordered the explusion of the Greeks from the towns of the lower Struma and the confiscation of all the revenues. Then in the winter of 1451 he sent orders all over his dominions to collect a thousand skilled masons and a proportionate number of unskilled workmen, who were to assemble early next spring at the site that he had chosen, at the narrowest part of the Bosphorus, just beyond the village then called Asomaton and now called Bebek, where a ridge justs out into the strait. The winter was hardly over before his surveyors were examining the ground and labourers began to demolish the churches and monasteries nearby, collecting from them such pieces of masonry as could be used again. His orders caused consternation at Constantinople. It was clear that this was the first move towards the siege of the city. . . . In June Constantine made his last effort to obtain from Mehmet an assurance that the building of the castle did not mean that an attack on Constantinople was to follow. His ambassadors were thrown into prison and decapitated. It was virtually a declaration of war.

Steven Runciman, 'The Fall of Constantinople', 1965

Castles in sunset

Emily gazed with melancholy awe upon the castle, which she understood to be Montoni's; for, though it was now lighted up by the setting sun, the Gothic greatness of its features, and its mouldering walls of dark grey stone, rendered it a gloomy and sublime object. As she gazed, the light died away on its walls, leaving a melancholy purple tint, which spread deeper and deeper as the thin vapour crept up the mountain, while the battlements above were still tipped with splendour. From those, too, the rays soon faded and the whole edifice was invested with the solemn duskiness of evening. Silent, lonely, and sublime, it seemed to stand the sovereign of the scene, and to frown defiance on all who dared to invade its solitary reign. As the twilight deepened, its features became more awful in obscurity; and Emily continued to gaze, till its clustering towers were alone seen rising over the tops of the woods, beneath whose thick shade the carriages soon after began to ascend.

The extent and darkness of these tall woods awakened terrific images in her mind, and she almost expected to see banditti start up from under the trees. At length the carriages emerged upon a heathy rock, and soon after reached the castle gates, where the deep tone of the portal bell, which was struck upon to give notice of their arrival, increased the fearful emotions that had assailed Emily. While they waited till the servant within should come to open the gates, she anxiously surveyed the edifice: but the gloom that overspread it allowed her to distinguish little more than a part of its outline, with the massy walls of the ramparts, and to know that it was vast, ancient and dreary. From the parts she saw, she judged of the heavy strength and extent of the whole. The gateway before her, leading into the courts, was of gigantic size, and was defended by two round towers crowned by overhanging turrets embattled where, instead of banners, now waved long grass and wild plants that had taken root among the mouldering stones, and which seemed to sigh, as the breeze rolled past, over the desolation around them. The towers were united by a curtain pierced and embattled also, below which appeared the pointed arch of a huge portcullis surmounting the gates: from these the walls of the ramparts extended to other towers overlooking the precipice, whose shattered outline, appearing on a gleam that lingered in the west, told of the ravages of war. Beyond these all was lost in the obscurity of evening.

Mrs Ann Radcliffe, 'The Mysteries of Udolpho', 1794

NOTES ON THE PLATES

1 Cumae was one of the most ancient of Greek colonies, having been founded from Chalcis about 1000 BC. It owes its fame to being the seat of one of the ten sibyls, or wise women. She pronounced her oracles in a subterranean chamber of which traces still survive, discovered as recently as 1932.

2 The fortified stronghold of Euryelus was built by Dionysus I, Tyrant of Syracuse in the years preceding and following 400 BC. It was one of the most elaborate military works of the Greek world and survives largely intact. There are five massive towers, protected by deep ditches hewn in the rock. Within the fort are numerous underground chambers used as magazines or storehouses, connected by passages.

3 The Lion Gate forms the ceremonial entrance to the city of Mycenae, and dates from the period of its enlargement about 1350–1330 BC. It is placed in a protective salient of the wall. The lintel, 6 feet thick, supports reliefs of two lions (or more probably lionesses) who rest their paws on two joined altars. They were probably an emblem of the ruling family, which the first excavators identified with that of Homer's Agamemnon.

4 Only the foundations remain of the *tholos* or rotunda of Epidauros, in Greece. There seem to have been six concentric walls (making it more complex than the similar structures at Delphi and Olympia), surrounded by an outer ring of twenty-six Doric columns. It was built between 360 and 320 BC and formed part of the precinct sacred to Asklepios.

5 The Temple of Khnum on Elephantine Island, Aswan, survives only as shattered fragments. Among the carvings is a depiction of Alexander the Great, shown as a pharaoh, doing homage to the ram-headed god Khnum.

6 Temple of Amun, Karnak. Every dynasty made its contribution to this great sacred site, which ended by becoming the grandest temple in the whole of Egypt. Its origins go back to the mid second millennium BC. The hypostyle hall is the work of Seti I and Ramesses II (1312–1301 BC). Other buildings went on being added until the time of Alexander.

7 In the same Iranian valley as that which holds the Achaemenid and Sassanian royal tombs (see pl. 31) is a strange angular building known as the 'Cube of Zoroaster'. Zoroaster is a semi-legendary figure who lived – if he lived at all – around 1000 BC. The religion associated with his name is based on a dualistic world-view, in which Good, in the person of Ahura-Mazda, is perpetually at war with Evil, called Ahriman. Ahura-Mazda's attribute is light, or fire, and the temple of Naqsh-e Rustam seems to have been built for fire-worshipping ceremonies.

8,9 The sacred precinct of Baalbek was one of the largest architectural complexes of the Roman Empire, in many of its features foreshadowing the Baroque. It consisted of a monumental entrance colonnade, two courts, one hexagonal, the other square, and two temples, dedicated to Bacchus and to Jupiter. The emperor mainly responsible was Antoninus Pius (AD 138–61), but it was altered by later Roman rulers as well as by Arabs and Turks. See also pl. 82.

10 Angkor Wat is a monument to the prosperity of the 12th-century kingdom of the Khmers. It is a vast temple to the Buddha and royal mausoleum, two and a half miles in circumference, and surrounded by canals and artificial lakes. Every surface is covered with reliefs showing divinities from Buddhist mythology. When the Khmer civilization fell, Angkor was reclaimed by the jungle, to be rediscovered only in the last century.

11,12 Chichén Itzá was built by the Toltecs, predecessors of the Aztecs, between the 6th and 10th centuries AD. It was a cult centre, not an inhabited city, and the rites which were practised there remain mysterious. It is certain, however, that they involved human sacrifice. The figure in the left-hand picture is the implacable Chacmool, who received the severed hearts of sacrificial victims.

13 Ukheidir, the 8th century palace of the Abbasid kings contains a mosque, audience halls, courts and living accommodation, all surrounded by a high wall of brick, pierced by gateways. Of the original four walls only two remain. On the outside towers alternate with blind arches; on the inside (shown here) the blind arches continue without interruption.

14 Spain is rich in Roman remains including some of the most spectacular aqueducts anywhere in the world. This 2nd-century AD road-marker is near one of them, crossing the valley of the Ebro outside Tarragona.

15 The Great Mosque of Kairouan is the major early Islamic building of North Africa. Begun in the 9th century, it was added to in the 11th and reached its present form in 1294. It consists of a huge open courtyard and a hypostyle hall resting on re-used classical columns.

16 Qasvin is an ancient town where traditional Muslim ways of life have survived the centuries.

17 S. Michele at Pavia, built in the early 12th century, is among the largest and best preserved Romanesque churches of North Italy. The flat façade has three doorways corresponding to the nave and two aisles. Their jambs are carved with foliage and vine-scrolls inhabited by charming griffins.

18 The early 12th-century porch of the abbey church of Moissac displays some of the most powerful sculptures of the Middle Ages. The sides are scalloped in a style clearly influenced by Moorish Spain. The central pillar or trumeau (right) is carved with lions and lionesses standing on each others' heads, and at the sides are strange elongated figures of saints in strained postures. Shown here, on the left, is St Peter with his two keys.

19 Apulia has a number of surviving Romanesque bronze doors. Those of Troia date from 1119–27, and include niello-work panels of saints (bottom two in this detail). The handles are held in the mouths of winged serpents.

20 The whole city of Fatehpur Sikri, between Delhi and Agra, was built by the Mughal Emperor Akbar in fulfilment of a vow (see pl. 187). Distinguished visitors left token horseshoes to be nailed to the city gate; among them was the Viceroy Lord Curzon, whose interest in Indian antiquities ensured the recording and preservation of this late 16th-century ghost town.

21 The panels of the bronze doors of S. Zeno, Verona, probably date from the 12th century, but have been rearranged at some point in their history. They show scenes from the Old and New Testaments and from the life of S. Zeno, who was a 4th-century bishop of Verona. This detail covers only the bottom of the right-hand door. Top row: a lion mask; and then two messengers from the Emperor Gallienus come to Zeno while he is fishing to persuade him to cure the Emperor's son, who is possessed by a demon. In the next row: Nebuchadnezzar throws Shadrach, Mishach and Abednego into the fiery furnace (only one of them is visible); and a waggoner is saved from being drowned in a flood by the intervention of S. Zeno. At the bottom: the sacrifice of Isaac (the Angel prevents Abraham from killing his son and points to the ram underneath him); and Noah inviting the animals into the Ark.

22 The panels of the bronze doors of Monreale Cathedral, also of the 12th century, are signed by Bonanus of Pisa. This detail shows the creation of Eve, Cain and Abel, and the Fall. Below, a vigorous heraldic griffin and lion.

23 These massive wooden doors were added in the 17th century to the Romanesque cathedral of Cefalù.

24 The palace of the Doria princes in Genoa was formed of two earlier palaces purchased by their ancestor Admiral Andrea Doria in 1521.

25 Gallipoli Cathedral, dating from the 17th century, has playfully classical decoration round the doorway and the two flanking niches.

26 This doorway in Cuzco belongs to the early days of the Spanish occupation. Note especially the coat of arms, the busts of illustrious members of the family, and the leaf-masks on the ends of the lintel.

27 Palladio built the Villa Maser for the Barbaro family, which included the famous humanist Daniele Barbaro. It might have been Daniele who devised the *trompe l'oeil* scheme of decoration

carried out by Paolo Veronese. In this view the door-frame is real, but everything else is painted, including the fictitious door round which the child is peeping.

28 The Ducal Palace at Mantua goes back to the Middle Ages, but was continuously altered and enlarged (one of its rooms was decorated by Mantegna: see pl. 154). This suite of rooms was decorated in the 18th century by Giuseppe Piermarini for the Empress Maria Theresa.

29 A medieval wall in Kairouan, made up of fragments taken from an ancient Roman site. The doorway consists of three deeply carved slabs that were probably once lintels.

30 The 'Temple of Diana' at Nîmes, built in the 2nd century AD, is now thought to have been not a temple but part of a palatial Roman baths. The alternation of segmental and triangular pediments was to be influential in both Romanesque and Renaissance architecture.

31 The whole valley of Naqsh-e Rustam is devoted to royal burials. Those of the Achaemenid kings (Darius and Xerxes) date from the 5th century BC. Six centuries later it was used again by Sassanid kings as a means of asserting the continuity of Persian civilization.

32 The structure of Palermo Cathedral belongs to the 12th and 13th centuries and the style is orthodox European Gothic, with a touch of Moorish influence (e.g. the wavy battlements). The clock tower was added in 1840.

33 The Palazzo dei Diamanti, Ferrara, was begun in 1493 by Biagio Rossetti for Sigismondo d'Este. The rustication in the form of diamonds has been claimed as an allusion to the diamond emblem of the Este family, but in fact it has parallels in other places, most notably in the exactly contemporary Faceted Palace in the Kremlin, Moscow, by Solari and Ruffo.

34 The Casa de las Conchas, Salamanca, was built in 1512–14, during the last and most lavish period of Spanish late Gothic. The plain wall-surface is ornamented with carved scallop shells (*conchas*), and both doors and windows are adorned with a wealth of foliated and cusped decoration.

35 Gaur is an ancient city in West Bengal, its antiquities slowly decaying in the lush jungle. This banded brickwork makes

striking use of the strong sunlight and shadow.

36 At Orvieto Cathedral alternating bands of black basalt and white travertine help to make up an almost abstract composition. The apsidal chapels are each given blank niches echoing the aisle windows in between. The cathedral's spectacular west front, finished in the mid-14th century, can be seen from this angle to be a mere screen, not corresponding to the building behind.

37 Netley, in Hampshire, was founded by Cistercian monks in the 12th century. Few of the details of the building survive. Many of the walls have become shapeless heaps of masonry, but fragments of a traceried window bear witness to its former glory.

38 Melrose Abbey was another Cistercian foundation. After destruction by the English, it was rebuilt in the early 15th century in a rich Decorated style showing signs of French influence. The south transept, shown here, has beautiful curvilinear tracery, once surmounted by a tier of statues, now lost.

39 Valencia. The practice of covering the fronts of houses with coloured tiles is an ancient Spanish tradition.

40 Sheik Safi was the founder of the Safavid Dynasty, and his mausoleum at Ardabil gathered the tombs of other members of the royal family until it comprised a whole complex of buildings. The brilliant tile mosaic which clothes every surface was added in the late 16th century.

41 A new west front was added to the old Romanesque church of S. Croce in Gerusalemme, Rome, in 1743. The work of Gregorini and Passalacqua, it has the monumentality of Neo-classicism, but its convex curve bears witness to the still vital Baroque.

42 The central square of Vigevano was laid out in the late 15th century by Bramante, and was the first attempt in Italy to create an architecturally unified urban space. In this detail the arcades pass in front of the old medieval fortress, effectively masking it – a slightly later alteration making the square even more vigorously unified. All the façades are covered with *trompe-l'oeil* painting.

43 Siena Cathedral, built between 1284 and 1380, is one of the most sumptuous creations of Italian Gothic. The façade was the last part to be completed, and is adorned with mosaic (mostly restored in the 19th century) and marble statues by Giovanni Pisano.

44 S. Michele, Lucca, embodies the Tuscan Romanesque style at its most lavish. The façade consists of superimposed storeys of dwarf arches, here inlaid with marble panels showing fabulous animals.

45 The screens on the windows of this wooden house are completely Islamic in their interplay of surface pattern, their segregation of space and their adaptation to sunlight and shadow.

46 S. Michele, Lucca (see pl. 44). This view exposes the 'dishonesty' of the façade, which suggests a far taller church than what actually exists.

47 This intriguing Neoclassical house at Piombino d'Ese, near Castelfranco, stands near a villa by Palladio.

48 The sumptuous façade of S. Pablo, Valladolid, dating from 1486–92, is so thickly encrusted with sculpted ornament that it is difficult to analyse into distinct parts. Typically for the Spain of Ferdinand and Isabella, secular and religious imagery are closely intermingled. Coats-of-arms held by angels press against the figures of saints and prophets in canopied niches.

49 Friday Mosque, Isfahan: the *mihrab* (prayer niche) is flanked by two *mimbars* (pulpits). The niche, covered with stucco combining foliage and calligraphy, dates from 1310. See pl. 55.

50 Kairouan. Typical of Islamic ornament is the way areas of pattern are enclosed in frames.

51 Built between 1650 and 1670, La Merced at Antigua was extensively repaired in the 18th century after an earthquake. The style is still that of Spanish Baroque, but with a naive vigour that almost suggests folk art.

52 The shrine of Pir-i Bakram, a Sufi mystic of the 14th century revered as a saint, was built soon after his death.

53 Kairouan. See pl. 15.

54 Mosque of Ibn Tulun, Cairo. See pl. 106.

55 The Friday Mosque at Isfahan has been called almost a textbook of Iranian styles, having been built, added to and altered from the 8th to the 17th centuries. The section seen here belongs to the Safavid period (16th century) when the brilliant blue glazed tilework was installed.

56 This worn wooden *mihrab* in a Tunisian mosque is, like all such prayer niches, a pointer to indicate the direction of Mecca, to which the worshipper must turn in prayer. The *mihrab* is traditionally the most richly decorated part of a mosque.

57, The temples at Bhuvaneshwar are among the most spectacular
59, Hindu remains in India. They date from the 7th century AD.
60 Within the sacred enclosure are extensive tanks (once filled with water from every holy stream and tank in India), many small temples, a Great Temple, and the Great Tower, 180 feet high. Like its near neighbour, Konarak, Bhuvaneshwar's glory is its sculpture; the exteriors are covered in intricate carving comprising abstract forms, floral and vegetal decoration and figures representing the pantheon of Hindu gods.

58 The cave temples of Badami were made between 550 and 650 AD. Walls, ceilings and columns are all carved out of the living rock, and are covered with reliefs showing the Hindu gods and scenes from their legends.

61 The decoration of the 17th-century palace of Amber in Rajasthan uses mirrors set inside stucco frames in the shape of plants – a superb combination of favourite Islamic themes (taken over from the Hindu Rajputs' rivals) transforming the interior into a magic cave.

62 The Alhambra occupies the top of a steep hill on the edge of Granada. Like most Islamic palaces it is a collection of small-scale buildings – halls, courtyards, baths, verandas – without a formal or unified plan. Its special qualities reside in the richness of its decoration (stucco and tile mosaic) and in its feeling of intimacy and withdrawal from the world. It was built mostly in the 14th century, and was occupied by the last Moorish dynasty in Spain up to 1492. This view shows a room looking out onto a small garden with a fountain.

63 The Temple of Apollo at Bassae (*c.* 450 BC) stands alone in a rocky landscape in the central Peloponnese. The ancient Greek writer Pausanias attributes its design to the architect of the Parthenon, Ictinus. The Doric *peripteros* or encircling colonnade is close to the Parthenon in style, but the interior of the *cella* incorporates several unusual features including the first recorded use of the Corinthian order.

64 A low ridge between the town of Agrigento and the sea bears the remains of four large Greek temples and fragments of others. Of

these, the Temple of Concord (*c.* 430 BC) is the best preserved, perhaps because it was converted into a church in the Middle Ages. It is an orthodox Doric temple with a total of thirty-four columns. Akragas was among the leading powers of Greek Sicily and was called 'the most beautiful city of mortals' by Pindar.

65 The identification of this building in Rome as a temple of Vesta is a modern guess which turned out to be wrong, though the name has stuck. Its real dedication is unknown. It was of Pentelic marble, built in the 1st century BC close to the ancient Forum Boarium and is based on a Hellenistic model. In the Middle Ages it was made into a church, dedicated first to St Stephen and then to the Virgin. Its entablature is missing and the roof is modern.

66 Bramante's 'little temple' at S. Pietro in Montorio was one of the first essays in Renaissance classicism, a variation on the theme of the Roman circular temple (compare pl. 65). The date is 1502–10. Bramante's intention was that the whole cloister should be transformed into a circle by the provision of a colonnade to match that of the Tempietto.

67, Monreale Cathedral combines Byzantine and Islamic influences.
68 The 12th-century cloister looks to contemporary Roman work for its inspiration. Small-scale colonnettes gaily decorated with Cosmati work (inlaid glass mosaic) are surmounted by twin capitals containing both figural and foliage carving.

69 The Court of the Lions is one of two large courts in the Alhambra, from which some of the most richly decorated rooms open (e.g. pl. 141). The twelve lions forming the fountain date from the 14th century.

70 The Temple of Horus at Edfu was built over several centuries. The part shown here was built by Ptolemy III in the late 3rd century BC. We are looking from inside the temple proper at columns covered with hieroglyphic inscriptions and topped by palm-leaf capitals.

71 This colonnaded hall at the ritual site of Chichén Itzá (see pls. 11, 12), flanking the Temple of the Warriors, was built by the Toltecs in the 10th century AD.

72 The cave shrines on the island of Elephanta were carved from the living rock in the 5th–8th centuries AD. Parts of the entrance, however, are constructed of masonry.

73 Angkor Thom, a temple only slightly smaller than Angkor Wat

302

(pl. 10), lies near to it in the Cambodian jungle. Here giant trees encroach upon the ruins.

74 Cambodia's grandest monuments are Angkor Wat and Angkor Thom (pls. 10, 73), but it has many smaller shrines, many dating from the days of the Khmer Empire and also swallowed up by the jungle. With Burma and Thailand, Cambodia is still one of the most solidly Buddhist countries in the world.

75 The Hoysaleshwara Temple at Halebid is dedicated to the Hindu god Shiva and his wife, Parvati. Each divinity's shrine is preceded by a pavilion containing a sculpture of the bull Nandi, Shiva's mount. The temple was built by King Vishnuvardhana in the 12th century AD. See also pl. 151.

76 The funerary temple of Ramesses III (1198–1166 BC) at Medinet Habu is particularly rich in carved scenes and hieroglyphic inscriptions. In plan it is a textbook example of the Egyptian temple: the entrance between massive pylons leads into the first of two open courtyards, with the enclosed temple proper at the end.

77 These attached columns modelled on the papyrus plant, with its faceted stem, decorate the North House at Saqqara, part of the huge funerary complex of King Djoser, of which the main feature is a stepped pyramid. The date is thought to be *c.* 2670 BC. Imhotep, the architect, was later hailed as a god.

78, Philippi was a thriving town in ancient Greece; it was the site of
79 the defeat of Brutus and Cassius by Octavius; its Early Christian community was sufficiently important to receive epistles from St Paul; and for over a thousand years it was the seat of a Byzantine metropolitan. These capitals are typically Byzantine in their stylized foliage forms and their covering of the surface with dense, deeply undercut ornament.

80 The Roman forum at Izmir (Smyrna) consisted of a courtyard measuring 395 × 260 feet, lined with double two-storeyed colonnades. The present remains date from a reconstruction after an earthquake of AD 178. In the centre was an altar to Jupiter.

81 The mosque in Jerusalem known as the Dome of the Rock stands on the site of Solomon's Temple, and is the oldest Islamic building in the world. It was built by Caliph Omar in 685, only fifty years after the death of Mohammed. The capital in the foreground is part of an arcade which crosses the top of the steps which lead up to the Dome. The capitals are Byzantine.

82 Temple of Bacchus, Baalbek. See pls. 8, 9.

83 The world of 11th-century iconography is lurid and often mysterious. Here at the church of Venosa in south-central Italy four lions stalk round the sides of the capital. Above them a fierce monster holds two small human figures by the legs.

84 The 12th-century portal of Ferrara Cathedral combines features from disparate cultures. The Atlas figure is ultimately Roman, but he rests incongruously on the back of a huge Persian lion with a bull's head between its paws.

85 The Vakil Mosque, Shiraz, was built between 1750 and 1770. The brick vaults rest on columns with twisted grooves and acanthus capitals.

86 Hadrian's Temple fronts the main street of Ephesus (pls. 182, 183). Its façade, a round arch flanked by two flat lintels, belongs to a type that was to be widely imitated, and forms the basis of the so-called 'Palladian window'. An inscription records that it was dedicated to the Emperor Hadrian, who reigned from AD 117 to 138.

87 The amphitheatre at Arles, although drastically restored, illustrates two of the key points of Roman architecture – the structural use of the round arch and the demotion of the orders to a purely ornamental use, as features applied to a standing façade.

88 The Basilica of Maxentius, begun by the last pagan emperor, Maxentius, and finished by the first Christian one, Constantine, in the 4th century AD, is among the largest classical buildings in Rome. Structurally it depends entirely on the semi-circular vault, the walls being merely a web filling the spaces beneath.

89 The triumphal arch of the ancient Roman city of Glanum survives near St Rémy-de-Provence. Its sculpture evokes the recent conquest of Trans-Alpine Gaul by Julius Caesar; it features four groups of captives, among them a woman.

90 The Arch of Septimius Severus in the Roman Forum was erected in AD 203 to commemorate the Parthian victories of the Emperor Septimius Severus and his sons Caracalla and Geta. Originally surmounted by a bronze chariot with six horses, it is one of the most elaborate of Roman triumphal arches, with three openings, columns on high pedestals and a wealth of relief carving.

91 Ukheidir. See pl. 13.

92 Blachernae Palace, Constantinople. In the 12th century the Byzantine emperors left the old palace near Hagia Sophia for more comfortable apartments higher up the Golden Horn. The fragmentary walls that survive up to a height of three storeys probably belong to the 13th century.

93 St Ambrose (Ambrogio) had made Milan one of the leading centres of Christianity in the 4th century AD. The monastery that he founded was rebuilt on a large scale between the 9th and 12th centuries, incorporating important architectural innovations. The cloister dates from about 1150, forming an atrium in front of the five-bay façade of the church.

94 The 12th-century mosaics in the nave of Monreale Cathedral illustrate stories from the Old and New Testaments. At the top, the Expulsion from the Garden of Eden and Adam and Eve labouring; at the bottom, the Flight into Egypt. See also pl. 138.

95 The columns and capitals at Gerace are re-used from classical buildings, as so often with Early Christian and Romanesque churches in Italy.

96 S. Stefano Rotondo, Rome, is essentially the circular central structure of a Roman market, adapted as a church in the 5th century and much reconstructed subsequently.

97 The Roman forum, Izmir. See pl. 80.

98 The famous 'Pont d'Avignon' across the Rhône was built in the 12th century, by St Bénézet, but the strong current damaged it repeatedly and it was abandoned in 1680. All that remains are four arches on the Avignon side.

99 The large Early Christian basilica at Aquileia was founded in the 4th century and rebuilt in its present form in the 11th. Here we are looking at the arches which span the transepts on either side of the chancel.

100 Hierapolis was a Hellenistic city founded by King Eumenes II of Pergamon. It became Roman in 133 BC, was largely destroyed by earthquake, rebuilt in the 1st century AD, and reached the height of its prosperity in the 2nd and 3rd centuries. The chief remaining buildings are the baths, a colonnaded street, a temple to Apollo, a

theatre and a Christian basilica dating from the 6th century, when Hierapolis became the seat of a bishopric.

101 The castle of Tarascon was built in the 12th century and enlarged in the 15th. After its military use was over, it became a prison, but has now been carefully restored and is one of the most complete castles in France. The moat is a channel of the River Rhône, on the bank of which it stands.

102 The monastery of Valle Crucis, founded by Cistercians in 1201, is small in scale but highly sophisticated architecturally. The elevation of the east end of the church is unusual in having narrow windows in the thickness of the buttresses.

103, Many of the best preserved Cistercian abbeys are in the Border
104 country between England and Scotland. Jedburgh was founded in the 12th century and from this period the choir of the church survives (foreground of pl. 103), with its highly unusual design of a gallery fitted between the large cylindrical piers of the main arcade. Beyond the crossing is the 13th-century nave. In pl. 104 we are looking in the same direction but from a point slightly to the left. The early Gothic pointed arches of the south aisle were originally covered by stone vaults of which only fragments remain.

105 Rievaulx was a 13th-century foundation, and its ruins are among the most perfect specimens of Cistercian Gothic in Europe. Here we are looking from the south transept of the church across the nave to the arcade on the other side. The multiple shafts and strong mouldings round the arches emphasize the tense linear quality of Gothic architecture, in contrast to the massive solidity of Romanesque.

106 At the Mosque of Ibn Tulun in Cairo the prayer-hall opens straight into the courtyard through an arcade. Its square piers with engaged columns in the corners are unusual and are copied from the earlier mosque at Samarra, in Iraq, where Ibn Tulun had lived. He founded this mosque, the earliest in Cairo, in 876.

107 The Khwaju Bridge, Isfahan, built by Shah Abbas in the 17th century, is a work not so much of engineering as of architectural fantasy. The river is not navigable and the base of the bridge forms a weir. All along it are pavilions and arcaded niches, for the citizens of Isfahan to linger and relax, and at the bottom, where the river flows over a series of steps, are platforms for people to sit actually surrounded by water.

304

108 Nerja. The large modern aqueduct brings water from the mountains to irrigate fields of sugar cane. Nerja is between Malaga and Granada.

109 The aqueduct of Roquefavour was built between 1842 and 1847 to carry water from the River Durance to the city of Marseilles.

110 The massive stone piers of the Shahrestan Bridge, Isfahan, go back to Sassanian times; the arches were rebuilt by the Seljuks in the 12th century.

111, 112   Qasvin. See pl. 16.

113 The observatory at Jaipur was built by the Rajput ruler Jai Singh II in the early 18th century. It is not an observatory in the modern sense (there were no telescopes in India at the time): its various giant instruments, one of them a sort of sextant, were designed to help fix the positions of the stars more exactly for astrological purposes.

114 The mosque at Damaghan is the oldest in Iran. It was initially built in the 8th century, soon after the coming of Islam to Persia, in a style that looks back to Sassanid architecture, and then rebuilt by the Seljuks in the 12th century.

115 Monreale Cathedral. See pls. 67, 68.

116 Hadrian's Villa at Tivoli, although called a villa because it was a country retreat, is in fact the largest palace in the Roman Empire, occupying an area of about seven square miles. Here Hadrian recreated in miniature the world of the Mediterranean through which he had spent his life travelling. An ancient writer says that 'he created in his villa at Tivoli a marvel of architecture and landscape gardening: to its different parts he assigned the names of celebrated buildings and localities, such as the Lyceum, the Academy, the Pryteneum, Canopus, the Stoa Poikile and Tempe, while in order that nothing should be wanting he even constructed a representation of Tartarus'. Canopus was a valley in Egypt with a shrine to the bull-god Serapis; in his reconstructed Canopus, Hadrian held ceremonies in the Egyptian style. Today its broken columns and arches have been restored, and a post-classical crocodile adds local colour.

117 Summer palace of S. Severino, Bino Favella, a comparatively little-known site, whose extensive remains deserve closer study.

118 The royal Sassanian palace, Ctesiphon, built by Chosroes I in the 6th century AD, consisted of a vast hall covered by a barrel vault and completely open at the end, flanked by two four-storey façades (one of which collapsed in 1909). The whole structure is of brick and the great arched vault, 83 feet in span and 120 feet high, surpassed even the achievements of imperial Rome.

119 S. Stefano del Bosco, Italy. The ruins of this once famous Carthusian monastery lie in a lonely valley in Calabria.

120 The great stupa of Ruanweli Dagoba at Anuradhapura is the oldest and one of the largest of the great stupas of Sri Lanka. It was built between 161 and 137 BC to hold relics of the Buddha. Stupas were originally burial mounds, but the form was taken up for the housing of sacred relics. Some historians have seen in it a symbolic representation of the cosmos. Many stupas attain enormous proportions, like artificial hills. Ruanweli was largely reconstructed during the early 20th century.

121 Varamin is now a village, but in the 13th and 14th centuries it was an important town and a regional capital. In the hot desert of this part of Iran the sun is excluded by thick windowless walls behind which are extensive shady interiors (sometimes forming large interconnecting spaces, such as bazaars) under many-domed roofs.

122 The Coptic monastery of Wadi el-Natrun, in an oasis on the edge of the Nile Delta, was founded in the 4th century. The oldest part is the church, in the right foreground, with its primitive domes surmounted by crosses.

123 The shrine of Hadrat-e Masumeh at Qom is one of the most sacred sites of the Shi'ite sect of Islam. Hadrat-e Masumeh died at Qom in AD 816. The splendid buildings that surround her tomb were erected under Safavid monarchs in the early 16th century, but its most prominent feature, the dazzling dome in the foreground, was covered with golden tiles as recently as the early 19th.

124 St Mark's, Venice. We are looking down from the top of the campanile on to the five domes of the cathedral. Its plan is Byzantine, the closest model being the now-destroyed church of the Holy Apostles in Constantinople. The interior is still basically of the 11th century, but the domes that we see from outside were added in the 13th century, providing a strong external accent.

125 The Mosque of Mohammad Ali in Cairo is essentially a Turkish building on Egyptian soil. Built between 1830 and 1848 by Mohammed Ali, newly independent (paradoxically) of Turkey, it follows the model of mosques in Istanbul, which goes back ultimately to Hagia Sophia. The huge central dome is supported by four semi-domes, with four smaller domes in the corners, creating a square interior. In the decoration it is the influence of European classicism that dominates.

126, The Taj Mahal, the mausoleum built by the Emperor Shah Jahan
127 for his favourite wife, Mumtaz Mahal, is justly famous as the masterpiece of Mughal architecture. Scale, design, materials and craftsmanship work together in perfect harmony. It was under construction between 1632 and 1634, and is made entirely of smooth white marble, giving an unearthly effect by moonlight. Inset into the marble are semi-precious stones forming decorative patterns and inscriptions. The central dome, beneath which the tomb rests, is flanked by four subsidiary domes, and the whole building stands on a raised platform with a minaret in each corner. On either side are mosques. In front, a long pool of still water reflects the variously shaped domes and towers in the changing light of morning, noon and evening.

128 The Great Mosque, Kairouan. See pl. 15.

129 The Mosque of Ibn Tulun, Cairo. See pls. 54, 106.

130 The whole group at Pisa of Cathedral, Campanile (the Leaning Tower), Baptistery and Campo Santo (cemetery) make up one of the most impressive architectural ensembles in Italy. The Baptistery is of two periods. The lower two storeys, with their arcades (the upper one a third the dimensions of the lower), belong to the 12th century. The original building then continued with another miniature arcade and a nearly-flat roof, through which penetrated a conical shape surmounting an interior dome. In the late 13th century this was covered up by an elaborate Gothic design incorporating a domical roof, but with the original cone still showing through at the top.

131 The Piazza S. Pietro, Rome. At the back rises the dome of St Peter's, designed by Michelangelo but only built after his death, possibly with some modifications, 1585–90. According to Michelangelo's intentions, the west front would have been directly in front of the dome, adding greatly to the effect of both, but this was lost when the nave was lengthened and the present west front built by Carlo Maderna in 1606–12. Fifty years later (1655–67), Bernini designed the great oval piazza with its double row of giant Doric columns, seen here in the foreground.

132 The dome of Florence Cathedral, equally remarkable for its engineering and for its style, stands at the beginning of the Italian Renaissance. By 1400 the Gothic cathedral had been completed up to the top of its walls, leaving a vast octagonal space over the crossing which no architect knew how to vault. Brunelleschi's solution, which he put into practice between 1420 and 1434, combined a pointed ribbed vault, essentially Gothic in structure, with bricklaying techniques and decorative motifs derived from ancient Roman buildings. The lantern on the top, which is purely classical in inspiration, was finished after his death in 1462.

133 Krak des Chevaliers is the best preserved of the Crusader castles of the Holy Land. It was built – 'a bone in the throat of the Saracens' – in the 12th century, and was designed to be self-supporting in the event of a siege. Apart from the spectacular fortifications, there are wells, store-rooms, barracks and living accommodation for the knights.

134 Pergamon was a Greek city later added to by the Romans. This vaulted passage shows the use of different stone for the side walls (partly buried in the earth) and the vault, whose small unsquared stones – no doubt originally covered by plaster – have given way in places.

135 The church of Stilo, built when this area of Italy was still open to Byzantine influence, could easily be mistaken for a village church in Greece. Its plan is a square divided into nine smaller squares. The centre is raised into a dome; the corners form four smaller domes and the four arms in between are covered by barrel vaults. All this is clearer from the exterior (pl. 157) than from inside.

136, Around Göreme in the ancient Cappadocia (central Turkey) is a
137 region of strangely shaped rock formations, which in Early Christian times became the home of communities of troglodite monks. Living in caves was until very recently common enough in parts of Anatolia, but few caves were as elaborate as these, with chapels, cells and refectories (and even their tables and benches) carved out of the living rock. Several of the churches have the Byzantine cross-in-square plan with four central columns (as at Stilo, pls. 135 and 157): among them are the two shown here. The Elmali Kilise or Church of the Ascension (pl. 137) carries the plan to a logical extreme, with domes over all nine compartments – a feat possible only in excavated, rather than constructed, architecture. These two churches were hollowed out of the same rock, probably around the same time, late 11th-early 12th century.

306

St Barbara (pl. 136) has retained its initial simple decoration, of abstract forms painted directly onto the rock; it has recently been shown that the motifs include Byzantine military standards and sceptres. At the Elmali Kilise this patterning was very soon (c. 1130?) overlaid with a coat of plaster and a complete scheme of sophisticated paintings, including Christ as Ruler of the World in the central dome (top), surrounded by the four Evangelists in the pendentives of the dome, figures of Old Testament prophets on the undersides of the arches, and the Ascension on the 'west' wall (bottom). This latter painting has been damaged, revealing the earlier consecration cross underneath.

138 The eastern apse of the cathedral of Monreale shows in the semi-dome Christ blessing; below him, the Virgin and Child flanked by angels and saints. See also pl. 94.

139 S. Maria Maggiore, one of the seven basilicas of Rome, dates essentially from the 5th century, but the mosaics of the apse, shown here, were installed at the end of the 13th (they are signed and dated – Jacopo Torriti, 1295). In the central circle the Virgin is crowned by Christ. Beside them saints and angels are grouped in adoration with the tiny figures of Pope Nicholas IV and Cardinal Jacopo Colonna kneeling in the foreground. Between the windows are three scenes from the life of the Virgin – the Nativity, the Dormition and the Adoration of the Magi. Below are four Renaissance reliefs by the Neapolitan Mino del Reame.

140 The Chapel of S. Zeno in the church of Sta Prassede, Rome, was built by Pope Paschal I in the early 9th century as a mausoleum for S. Zeno and a host of early martyrs as well as for his own mother. It is tiny, dimly lit and entirely covered with mosaic and marble veneer. In the dome four angels hold aloft a disc containing the half-figure of Christ. In the niche below are four female figures: Paschal's mother Theodora (who has a square halo and the inscription 'Theodora Episcopa'), Sta Prassede, the Virgin and (probably) St Anne.

141 Vault of the Sala de las Dos Hermanas (Hall of the Two Sisters) in the Alhambra, Granada. The muqarnas vault, made up of small concave segments, variously called 'honeycomb' or 'stalactite', is an Islamic speciality, but nowhere carried to such splendid lengths as in this small room, probably part of the queen's apartments.

142 In the former Great Mosque, now the Cathedral, of Córdoba, this vault covers the bay in front of the mihrab, or prayer-niche, and is the most elaborately decorated part of the building. Eight

intersecting arches leave an octagonal space in the centre, intricately adorned with mosaics. The date is 10th century.

143 The dome of the Chapel of the Holy Shroud, Turin Cathedral, built by Guarino Guarini between 1667 and 1690, is without parallel. Over a triangle of arches (symbolizing the Trinity) he places a round dome with six windows, the heads of which are connected by six segmented arches. These arches in turn support another six arches, and so on, diminishing in scale, until the lantern is reached, when they sprout twelve free-standing ribs holding up a circle which frames the dove of the Holy Ghost.

144 S. Giovanni dei Fiorentini, the church of the Florentines in Rome, was begun in the 16th century to a design by Antonio da Sangallo the Younger, but not finished until 1614. The building is cruciform and the dome stands over the crossing.

145 S. Maria in Campitelli, Rome, is the masterpiece of Carlo Rainaldi, under whom it was built in the 1660s. This dome is not over the crossing but over the choir, giving an unusual spatial quality to the interior. Rainaldi was not tempted by the eccentric daring of contemporaries such as Bernini, Borromini and Guarini (pls. 143, 147). His dome is of the orthodox Renaissance type, the coffered cupola resting on a low drum pierced by circular windows. Nor do the details stray far from orthodoxy, the whole design looking forward to the classical style of the next century.

146 The dome of S. Carlo ai Catinari, Rome, 1611–46, by Rosato Rosati, is again in the orthodox Renaissance tradition relatively unaffected by the Baroque. Each element, however, is enriched with gilding and ornament, and the coffering of the dome, with its diminishing circles, gives the impression of lightness and elegance. The church is unaisled and relatively small, the dome covering the whole interior.

147 S. Lorenzo in Turin (1668–87) by Guarino Guarini, has a dome that matches his Chapel of the Holy Shroud (pl. 143) in originality and bravura. Its most likely derivation is from an Islamic vault of the type used at Córdoba (see pl. 142). Here too eight arches intersect to form a central octagon, but in a more complicated way, each rib overlapping two sets of springers. The whole design is further transformed by the fact that the spaces between the ribs are left open, with light glimpsed through a variety of oddly shaped apertures. Inside the central octagon the whole process is repeated more simply (closer to the Córdoba pattern), with light this time coming from the sides.

148 The dome of S. Ivo della Sapienza, the university church of Rome, by Borromini, 1642–50. Here the plan consists of two interpenetrating equilateral triangles, the points of one triangle being given concave curves, those of the other convex. The result is a typically Baroque rhythm, only resolved in the circular oculus at the top.

149 The cathedral of Cuenca was built in the years around 1200, when Spanish architecture was dominated by French Gothic: note here the sexpartite vault and the slender shafts with stiff-leaf capitals. The lavish Renaissance wrought-iron grille by Hernando de Arenas (1557), however, is characteristically Spanish.

150 The Friday Mosque, Isfahan: a detail of the *muqarnas* vault so typical of Islamic architecture everywhere (see pl. 141). This is one of the great porches, or *iwans*, that open from the main courtyard. See pl. 55.

151 Carved stone ceiling of the Hoysaleshwara Temple, Halebid. See pl. 75.

152 The nave of S. Giovanni Evangelista, Parma, was built in a Gothic style between 1498 and 1510. Some forty years later the ribs were decorated with Renaissance paintings of the type based on ancient Roman murals and popularized by Raphael. Putti, satyrs and allegorical figures like Father Time pursue their various activities among plants, eagles, umbrellas and scrolls.

153 The banded stonework of Orvieto Cathedral has already been seen on the exterior in pl. 36. Over the nave there is no stone vault or painted ceiling, but the timber frame open to the roof.

154 In his decoration of the ceiling of the Camera degli Sposi in the Ducal Palace at Mantua, 1464–74, Andrea Mantegna was the first to use the newly perfected science of perspective to create the effect of looking up from below (Italian *di sotto in sù*) into a fictitious space existing overhead. Here several women and their black servant seem to be peering down at us over a circular parapet. They are accompanied by a peacock and little winged cherubs, three of whom are standing dangerously on our side of the balustrade. At one point a stick has been laid across the opening, on which a tub with a plant in it balances precariously, threatening every moment to fall upon us.

155 The garden room of the Villa Cicogna, near Lake Lugano, was decorated in the 16th century by the Campi brothers from

Cremona. In the ceiling the theme of the garden is continued by the representation of plants and animals seen through a trellis, an idea apparently invented by Leonardo da Vinci much earlier in nearby Milan.

156 The ceiling of S. Ignazio, Rome, by Andrea Pozzo (1685), is the most ambitious of all *sotto in sù* paintings, executed by a man who was equally eminent as a mathematician and as a painter (he was also a Jesuit priest). In meticulous foreshortening an elaborate structure of classical columns and arches rises above us, leading the eye to Heaven itself, which opens to receive the glorified St Ignatius, founder of the Jesuit Order. At the sides of this detail are personifications of two of the Four Continents, where Jesuit missionary zeal had won new converts to Christianity: on the left, Africa wearing a diamond on her brow and carrying an elephant's tusk; on the right, America who wears a feather headdress.

157 Stilo. See pl. 135.

158 The octagonal cathedral of Split was originally the mausoleum of the Roman Emperor Diocletian, and indeed the whole of the old town of Split is contained within his immense palace. The photograph is taken from the adjoining campanile, built in the 13th century.

159 S. Teodoro, Rome. This small round church goes back to the 6th century but has been repaired and restored many times since.

160 Italian roofscape, photographed from a window in the castle of Roccasinibalda, about thirty miles north-east of Rome.

161, 162 Mandalay is the centre of a whole area of Buddhist temples and shrines, one precinct being known as 'the Seven Hundred and Thirty Pagodas'. The most spectacular is the Arakan Pagoda, dating from the late 18th century. It contains a venerated bronze image of the Buddha. According to the ancient legend quoted in the standard guide to Burma (Murray's *Handbook*, 1959), 'the image was originally set up during the lifetime of the Great Master. The utmost skill and most persistent energy had failed in fitting the parts together, till the Buddha, perceiving from afar what was going on, and ever full of pity, came himself to the spot, and embracing the image seven times, so joined together the fragments that the most sceptical eye cannot detect the points of junction. So like was the image, and so sublime the effulgence which shone around during the manifestation, that the reverently gazing crowd could not determine which was the model and which was the Master.'

163 Macao, the old Portuguese trading post off the coast of China, contains buildings in every style. Here the typical pagoda roofs follow the Chinese tradition.

164 Banteai Srei lies deep in the Cambodian jungle about fourteen miles from Angkor Wat (pl. 10). Built in AD 1304, it was one of the last works of the great Khmer kings before the collapse of their empire. Shown here are the tops of two of a series of false doors. The elaborate crests are formed by *nagas*, water-spirits with cobra hoods.

165 Nikko is the chief secular shrine of Japan. Built in the early 17th century on the orders of Tokugawa Ieyasi, whose burial place it is, it comprised a galaxy of splendid buildings. It has been calculated that six acres of gold leaf was used in the decoration. This detail is from the Yomeimon, or Gate of Sunlight, a two-storeyed structure covered with dragons, lions and clouds.

166 The Golden Pavilion at Kyoto belongs to the Muromachi period; originally built as the villa of a nobleman, it was turned into a temple soon after 1400. The original structure has been repeatedly rebuilt, most recently after its complete destruction by fire in 1955. It is, however, an exact copy of the medieval building.

167 Path at Cumae. See pl. 1.

168 The theatre at Palmyra is a typical Hellenistic theatre, the stepped seats arranged in sections divided by aisles, the centre separated from the audience by a low stone wall (so that it could be flooded for aquatic shows), and a row of columns encircling the back.

169 Epidauros, in Greece, is an ancient sanctuary dedicated to Apollo, of which the theatre is the largest and best preserved feature. (For the *tholos* see pl. 4.) It is also notable for being the only Greek theatre to retain its circular *orchestra*, or acting area. Here we are looking through one of the side entrances (*parodoi*) across the *orchestra* towards the tiers of seats.

170 The sanctuary of Apollo at Didyma, on the western coast of Turkey, was the largest structure in the Hellenistic world, but it was not a temple in the normal architectural sense. Everything was on a vast scale. It was surrounded by a double row of huge Ionic columns (only two of which remain to their full height), within which rose the walls of what would conventionally be the *cella*. This, however, was so large that it could not be covered by a roof and was therefore left as an enclosed court, open to the sky. The photograph shows the flight of steps leading to the portico.

171 Persepolis was the ceremonial capital of the Persian Kings Darius and Xerxes. In 330 BC Alexander captured it and deliberately destroyed it, but impressive vestiges still remain, notably this staircase carved with the figures of guards and tribute-bearers, witnesses to the glory of the Achaemenid monarchy.

172 This monumental staircase in the citadel of Yapahuwa, built *c.* 1280 AD, led to a temple containing a tooth of the Buddha. Its sides are marked by guardian animals, including lions and elephants and a hybrid that combines both. The source of this exotic style is still uncertain. Some elements are South Indian, some medieval Sinhalese, and some Indo-Chinese.

173 The Scala dei Giganti in the Ducal Palace, Venice (so-called because of Sansovino's giant statues of Mars and Neptune that stand at its top), leads up from the courtyard to the principal rooms on the first floor. It was built about 1500 after a fire destroyed most of the palace in 1483. Every step is inlaid with a different pattern.

174 Sumerian, Babylonian and Assyrian ziggurats, unlike the pyramids of Egypt, were not tombs but artificial hills upon whose summits were shrines to the gods. The ziggurat of Choga Zambil near Susa, built of sun-dried brick in the 13th century BC, preserves its ceremonial gateway and part of its staircase to the top.

175 Courtyard of the *ribat*, or barracks, of Sousse, completed in 821, when the 'Holy War' for the expansion of Islam was still a living movement. Note the Kufic inscription along the top of the wall.

176 Palazzo Doria-Pamphili, Genoa, 1521–29: characteristic of Renaissance Genoa is this type of palace entered by a vestibule from which a flight of steps leads up to an open arcaded courtyard.

177 Staircase of the Palazzo del Quirinale, Rome, begun in 1583 by Ottaviano Mascarino for Pope Gregory XIII. The oval plan, used here for the first time for a staircase, was to be one of the most favoured Baroque forms.

178 Another oval staircase, this time in the Palazzo Boncampagni at Vignola. The palace was built in the late 16th century; the staircase, added at a slightly later date, is by Bartolomeo Tristino.

179 The Jardin de la Fontaine at Nîmes was laid out in the 18th century, taking advantage of natural springs and a series of basins, some of which went back to Roman times. With its combination of water, architecture and landscape, it suggests the setting of a *fête galante* in one of Watteau's delicately nostalgic paintings.

180 The Yeni Valide Mosque, Istanbul, was built during the late 16th and early 17th centuries. Its architect was Davut Ağa, a younger contemporary of the great Sinan. His mosques continue Sinan's style, but they lack his originality and inventiveness. This one is virtually a copy of Sinan's Şehzade Mosque in the same city.

181 The Via Sacra, or 'Sacred Way', led through the centre of the Roman Forum, skirting many of the major buildings such as the Basilica of Constantine, the Basilica Julia and the Atrium of the Vestal Virgins, to end at the Triumphal Arch of Tiberius.

182, The Marble Road of Ephesus ran through the ancient city from the
183 Temple of Artemis to the harbour, changing direction and following the rise and fall of the land. It was lined with monumental buildings, including the Temple of Hadrian (pl. 86), but retained the human scale and an element of informality in its planning. For part of the way it had colonnaded sidewalks.

184 The piazza of Nemi, a medieval town in the Alban Hills near Rome. Typical of Italian hill towns is the steep variation in levels, with ramps and steps connecting one part to another.

185 A Roman floor mosaic plays tricks with perspective. The putto carrying flowers is represented as if seen frontally, but the surrounding pattern is portrayed like a ceiling seen from below.

186 S. Clemente is perhaps the most historically interesting of all the churches of Rome. Underneath the present church are two other levels. The lowest and earliest is a Roman temple to Mithras with an Early Christian house church next to it. Above that are the extensive remains of an early 4th-century basilica built by Constantine. In 1084 Constantine's building was destroyed by the Normans; it was filled in and the present church built on top of it, incorporating some of the furnishings that were salvaged. These include the stone screens and the two pulpits on either side of the photograph. The canopy at the end and the very fine inlaid marble pavement date from the time of Pope Paschal II, early 12th century.

187 In Mughal architecture light itself became an element in the design. Here a polished marble floor, inlaid with an intricate pattern of interlacing foliage, is dappled by another pattern coming through the lacy screens (each one a single piece of carved white marble), and moving with the moving sun. The little building is

the tomb of the Muslim hermit Shaikh Salim Chishti, who had foretold the birth of a son to Akbar. The town built by the Emperor around the site of his hermitage (*c.* 1569–74) was soon abandoned, chiefly for lack of water.

188 The Phoenicians have left few physical remains, although it was they who invented the alphabet and originated writing as we know it. Byblos, which gave the Greek language its word for 'book', during the 2nd millennium BC was a large and flourishing port. Philo called it 'the oldest city in the world', and the ancient Egyptians imported cedars of Lebanon from here. The chief goddess was Astarte, and these stelae were probably associated with her worship.

189 S. Apollinare in Classe, Ravenna, dates from the 6th century, but its brick campanile was added in the 10th, in a plain Romanesque style. As it rises the number of openings increases.

190 Orvieto is built on a high outcrop of rock, and in order to obtain water it was necessary to dig down more than 200 feet. The enormous Pozzo di S. Patrizio (St Patrick's Well), 43 feet wide, was partly dug, partly constructed of masonry, by the Florentine architect Antonio da Sangallo. It has two separate spiral staircases which never meet. Asses went down one and returned up the other carrying water.

191 The tall brick belltower of S. Maria in Cosmedin, Rome, with its tiers of triple arches, was built *c.* 1200. The columns in the foreground belong to the 'Temple of Vesta' (pl. 65).

192 The 13th-century campanile of Siena Cathedral is clearly of the same type as that in the previous photograph, but just as at Ravenna (pl. 190) the number of openings increases with the height. Like the cathedral itself, of which we see the central dome, the campanile is built of light and dark stone in horizontal stripes.

193 Milan Cathedral is almost the only major building in Italy to use the fully developed Gothic style as understood in the north – a style of stone rib-vaulting, flying buttresses and large windows full of tracery, together with a whole repertoire of pinnacles, gables and dense sculptural ornaments. Here we are looking towards the crossing, with the choir and transept on either side. The building was begun at the end of the 14th century, and a whole series of architects worked on it, many from France, Germany and Flanders.

194 The church of Nuestra Señora del Pilar (Our Lady of the Pillar) at Saragossa is like no other church in the world. It is a huge rectangular building, the latest of a series of shrines to hold a little image of the Virgin or a marble pillar said to have been placed here by St James. She is dressed in a rich cape that is changed every day. The church was begun in 1681; its strange silhouette is due to the large central dome, the ten smaller domes and the tall minaret-like towers in each corner, the last of them finished only about 1970.

195 The crossing tower of Burgos Cathedral, Spain, was the last part of the cathedral to be built and one of the last great works of Gothic architecture. It was completed in 1567 and bears the arms of Charles V, but still shows few traces of the coming Renaissance (though note the fluted columns standing against each of the eight corners and the balustrades running round at two levels).

196 The Great Mosque at Samarra was built in the 9th century. We are looking out through a gap in the ruined enclosure wall to the spiral-ramped minaret, the oldest minaret in the Islamic world. It is tempting to see in it a descendant of the ancient Mesopotamian ziggurat, a symbolic mountain leading to heaven.

197 The Bupaya Pagoda at Pagan, Burma, was built by an early king, probably in the 3rd century AD. An English traveller in 1855 observed that it was 'like a great pumpkin with the thick end uppermost, a simple spire rising from the top and a succession of concentric sloping walls and parapets crowned with trefoils'. Before its destruction by Kubla Khan in the 13th century, the great city of Pagan extended twenty miles along the Irrawaddy River and boasted some 13,000 pagodas (see also pl. 201).

198 The tomb of Mir Muhammad on Khark Island belongs to a local style characteristic of the 9th century. The tall faceted dome is often called a sugar-loaf because of its resemblance to the white solid sugar sold in Iranian grocery shops. Khark Island is at the north end of the Persian Gulf near Bushehr.

199 The half-finished church of the Sagrada Familia (Holy Family) in Barcelona, begun in 1884, is a monument both to the genius of its architect, Antoni Gaudí, and to the patriotic pride of the Catalans, for whom it is a symbol. We are looking at the façade of the north transept, with the chancel on the left. The style clearly derives ultimately from Gothic, but greatly modified by Gaudí's feeling for organic forms and fondness for unusual materials. Work on the corresponding spires of the other transept is now

complete and the whole church should be finished by the end of the century.

200 Buddhist pagodas at Mandalay. See pls. 161, 162.

201 The Mahabodhi Pagoda at Pagan, built in the early 13th century, is unique in Burmese architecture in being closely modelled on an Indian prototype, the venerable temple at Bodh Gaya that stands next to the Bodhi tree, where the Buddha received enlightenment. The vast sacred site of Pagan (see also pl. 197) was recently severely damaged by an earthquake.

202 Wat Phra Jetupon (popularly known as Wat Po), founded in 1793, is the largest Buddhist monastery in Bangkok. Its buildings have been extended many times, and now include hundreds of galleries, towers, temples and shrines.

203 The Rifai Mosque in Cairo was begun in the mid-19th century by the daughter-in-law of Mohammed Ali (see pl. 125); abandoned after her death, it was completed in 1906–11 by the scholarly German architect Herz. Its style is that of 14th-century Mameluke buildings in Cairo, with a ribbed dome and massive minarets of which each tier has a different form; also distinctively Egyptian are the angular-headed niches in the lower stages of the minarets. The mosque became the royal mausoleum; among those buried are King Farouk and, most recently, the Shah of Iran. It stands next to the Mosque of Sultan Hassan, from which it is seen here.

204 The fortress of Rumeli Hisar on the Bosphorus was built by Sultan Mehmet II in 1452, as part of his plan to isolate and besiege Constantinople. Its mighty walls and towers achieved their purpose. The city fell a year later.

205 The Aljafería at Saragossa is a complicated building, begun as a palace by the Moors, transformed into a monastery by the Christians, and taken over as a royal residence in the 14th century. During the siege of Saragossa by the French in 1809 it was seriously damaged, but then restored for use as a barracks, prison and arsenal. It is the setting of Verdi's *Il Trovatore*.

206 The castle of Los Viveros at Fuensaldaña, near Valladolid, is a reminder of the days when the region was the front line of the Reconquista, the seemingly endless war against the Moors. It was begun in the 13th century; the imposing keep with its six towers, battlements and machicolations, dates from the 15th century.

207 Erice (the ancient Eryx, medieval Monte San Giuliano) is at the very westernmost tip of Sicily. From here on a clear day the coast of Africa can be seen. The town is basically medieval. Its castle, now mostly ruined and for long used as a prison, stands on a precipitous cliff and was virtually unassailable.

208 The Alcázar (Citadel) of Segovia rises like a fairy-tale castle on a steep rock at one end of the city. Although very ancient (it was founded by the Moors, then enlarged and reconstructed by the Kings of Castile in the 15th and 16th centuries), its present romantic appearance is very largely due to a restoration after a fire in 1862. Today it houses military archives.

209 Jaisalmer, in Rajasthan, was the capital of a Hindu Rajput clan. Now abandoned, its double line of fortifications, evidence of the wars that accompanied the Mughal conquest of India, are largely intact and are among the best examples of Hindu military architecture.

210, On the opposite bank of the River Rhône from the town of
211 Avignon (and once connected to it by the famous bridge, pl. 98) lies Villeneuve-lès-Avignon. Fort St André, whose massive two-towered gateway is shown here, was built by Louis VIII and Philippe le Bel of France as a bastion against the Counts of Provence, whose domain began at Avignon. The walls surround what was originally the abbey of St André. Villeneuve was taken over by the popes during the papal exile and many cardinals and officials made their homes here.

INDEX

Numbers in *italics* refer to the plates and
to the Notes on the plates